Reiki
and
Your Intuition

A Union of Healing and Wisdom

BOOK 2 IN THE REIKI HEALING SERIES

Tina M. Zion

Published in the United States by WriteLife Publishing
(An imprint of Boutique of Quality Books Publishing Company, Inc.)
www.writelife.com

Printed in the United States of America

978-1-60808-213-1 (p)
978-1-60808-214-8 (e)

Library of Congress Control Number: 2019901319

Book and cover design by Robin Krauss, www.bookformatters.com
Cover artwork by Corey Ford, www.coreyfordgallery.com
Toroidal Field illustration by Jacqueline Rogers, www.jacquelinerogers.com
Editor: Olivia Swenson

I dedicate this book to the Reiki healers who have shared their personal stories here and to each reader who creates their own story by opening all their pathways for Reiki healing and intuitive wisdom to surge through them.

Praise for Tina M. Zion

and

Reiki and Your Intuition - A Union of Healing and Wisdom

Reiki and Your Intuition: A Union of Healing and Wisdom is a valuable tool for personal and spiritual growth through the practice of Reiki. It provides the Reiki community with a wonderful resource, supporting students and practitioners alike in the understanding that intuition is a key part of the personal healing experience. Tina takes us step-by-step through the development of our intuition and awareness, laying to rest for good the question of whether intuition belongs in our Reiki practice.

"It is our light that guides other from darkness" — In her gentle and nurturing style, which students around the world will instantly recognize, Tina empowers us to embrace and develop our intuition whilst avoiding the interpretations of our thinking mind.

— Mary Hambly
Reiki Teacher and Practitioner
Founder of Emurge Life Coaching
Editor of *The Reiki News* (Reiki New Zealand, Inc.)

Tina Zion, in her new book *Reiki and Your Intuition*, has once again proven herself to be a consummate teacher of Reiki and Intuition. In this latest book she expands the definition of Reiki as a technique to enhance our understanding of how Reiki energy opens the way to a limitless experience of healing energy. As always, she emphasizes respect and honoring of the sacred trust inherent in being a Reiki practitioner. In this book, she includes rich personal first hand experiences of other Reiki practitioners and how Reiki has affected their life and practice. Even though she is addressing students and practitioners of Reiki, there is valuable information for anyone wishing to enhance their intuitive skills. Her deep love and respect for Reiki will be instilled into any student or potential student who reads the book. Written in a voice that is heartfelt and authentic, I wholeheartedly recommend this book.

— Helen Pankowsky, M.D.
Inspired Life Psychiatry www.helenpankowskymd.com
and author of *Living Aware & Inspired*

Tina Zion has produced another clearly written, easy to understand progressive book on the healing energies of Reiki. She was born into a family of fourth generation mediums and this, together with her strong intuitive abilities, her passion and enthusiasm to teach the art of Reiki to students in all parts of the world, is the foundation of her courses and training sessions. Tina's passion for teaching Reiki and sharing her extensive knowledge flows through the pages of this new book and helps to further bridge the gap between science and spirituality. The courses held in New Zealand are very enthusiastically attended.

— Joan Hetherington
Reiki Master: Reiki NZ Member
Full Healer Member: National Federation of Spiritual Healers NZ
(Trained in the UK)

Other Books by Tina M. Zion

The Reiki Teacher's Manual
Become a Medical Intuitive
Advanced Medical Intuition

Foreword

When I became a Master Teacher in the Reiki energy, I was a very novice beginner and I remember searching the Internet for any reading material that would help me develop my own personal style of teaching. This was when I first stumbled upon Tina Zion's Reiki Master Teacher's Manual. Wow! It blew me away. It was just what I needed, a practical manual that set out a perfect style of teaching that was simple and easy to follow.

Tina's book helped me gain trust in myself and my teaching abilities. So much so that it prompted me to write to the Author, something I had never done before, expressing my thanks for making available such a clear and practical guide. As a result, a friendship was formed that has spanned quite a few years and opened dooorways for both of us.

I remember getting a very clear impression when I sent off the email to Tina that first time that this would be the beginning of an intense period of learning for me and that eventually Tina would visit New Zealand. Why I got that clear impression was a mystery to me then. How and why would a lady from the States ever deem to visit the little country called New Zealand that was so far removed from the rest of the World! I dismissed that image and put it down to my "imagination." Since them, I have learned to trust my "imagination."

From this humble beginning I became deeply involved in the Reiki movement in New Zealand, through Reiki NZ Inc. and this enabled me to be instrumental in inviting Tina to visit New Zealand and to be blessed with her attendance at two very successful Reiki International Conferences run by Reiki NZ Inc. where she was well received in sharing her vast knowledge with us.

Through Tina's teachings I have learned to trust my intuition more and more. Now seeing all this information put down in another of Tina's books opens up a wealth of useful and practical information that I have come to expect from a gifted and genuine author such as Tina Zion.

For me, this is the best book Tina has written so far. In fact, it feels as though I have been waiting for such a book because it answers many of the questions that have been on the edge of my mind for so long. It is not only a book to pick and read but a practical manual that draws you in to participate, explaining and encouraging you to explore your own mind and to make practical adjustments to your understanding of the truth of your intuition and the unconditional love within yourself. This book helps affirm the reality that intuition and Reiki are not separate from each other but are part and parcel of the whole. "Intuition is simply information within and from the life force of the Universe."

The personal stories that are included in this book are inspiring and encouraging, adding a new depth to each chapter. Sharing that information with readers in such a practical and informative way transforms the unusualness of different situations of healing, putting the practitioner at ease with accepting the situations, taking away the fear that we may be doing something "wrong" to receive such information. I remember sharing something with one of my students once and she remarked that I made it seem so "normal." The relieved look on her face showed the value of such stories.

I know this book will become a "Recommended Reading" book for many students, not only for Reiki people but for anyone who wishes to develop and grow through their intuition. Thank you Tina Zion for writing such a book as this for all of us to share in. It is now up to each reader to discover the easy and practical knowledge it contains.

Happy reading.

Erica Sabbage
Reiki Master Teacher
Intuitive Reader
Northland, New Zealand

Contents

Part One

Intuition: What Is It All About?

CHAPTER 1

Reiki Opens New Doorways

My toes feel the deep rich grass. The sun warms my back. I look down and see a large black fish swim past in the deep pool, and when I look up I see the famous Tor at the top of the tallest steep hill. I am sitting in the sacred grounds of King Arthur's grave at Glastonbury, England.

I travel around the globe because of Reiki. I have a voice because of Reiki. I am a vessel of energy and words that are not mine. I teach about intuition, medical intuition, and intuitive Reiki. People seem to appreciate the information and the laughter that comes through me. I am free, strong, confident, and vital because of the brightest Light of Reiki running through my physical body and my energetic soul. This is just a split second about my life. This is just an example of where Reiki will take you if that is where you want to go.

Reiki tends to blast doors open in our physical world, and at the same time it blows off doors that hinder or block the intuitive healer within you. Begin by exploring the intuitive you and the Reiki healer within. What do you want to do? What do you want to become? What are you meant to do in the current life that you have right now? What dreams keep popping up and repeating no matter what else you are doing? Where do you want to go in your current life? The word "where" does not necessarily mean a certain geographical place. It could mean a certain direction of thinking, an achievement, an award, a goal, or a level of awareness. It could mean achieving a certain level of knowledge, a certain certificate, or a wisdom. It could be about you becoming the Reiki healer you are meant to become.

YOUR MOMENT OF

Self-Awareness

Let your expanded awareness begin right now. What are the key words, thoughts, or images that are leaping into your mind as you read these words? Write down the details in your awareness.

_____

_____

_____

_____

Notice already that this is more than just another Reiki book. This is a step-by-step process for exploring your heart and soul as Reiki touches your life, enters your experience, and becomes an integral part of who you are. I now offer this book as the next step to assist you, as a practitioner or a teacher, in understanding all the strange and sometimes weird and scary intuitive perceptions that Reiki opens us up to. My intent for this manual is to provide a clear and knowledgeable framework that assists you, as a healing vessel, in creating a beautiful union between healing and intuitive wisdom.

Intuition and Reiki

Intuition is a deep concern within the massive worldwide community of Reiki practitioners. People trained in the hands-on energy healing called Reiki have interestingly placed themselves within one of two groups. One group adamantly states that intuition has no place in Reiki healing sessions, while the other group declares that it is impossible to stop intuitive awareness from happening while offering Reiki.

I was completely pumped up and feeling excited, happy, and energized when I declared to a group of medical intuitive students, "Reiki will blast open any limiting blockages. Your closed gates will swing wide open, and you will enter into new realms of learning and new levels of wisdom. Your intuition will pop open! You will walk with one foot in the physical and one foot in the non-physical. Reiki blasts open your natural intuitive skills!"

A firm, deep female voice from the back row had her own announcement. She declared, "You are never to receive intuition while you are giving Reiki!"

I calmly responded, "Why do you say that?"

"My Reiki instructor always tells everyone that intuition has no place in a Reiki session."

I was not alarmed at what she was saying. I was alarmed at how distraught the medical intuitive student was. She looked as if she was struggling and suffering while sitting in a three-day medical intuitive intensive workshop. She was literally and figuratively sitting in the midst of her struggles.

A year later, a student in a different medical intuition class stated, "I am getting so much intuitive information while I am doing Reiki sessions that I am confused. I am overwhelmed, and I do not know what to do. I am about to stop doing Reiki because I am in such conflict. I do not know if this is part of Reiki or if I am doing it wrong. Should I be receiving intuitive information about my client or should I push it aside or should I just stop doing Reiki sessions? To be truthful I have decided to just stop offering Reiki!"

Who will these students believe, me or their Reiki teachers? Who should they trust, me or the other teachers? How will the students sort through the anguish I see on their faces? The answer to my questions is simple: each of you needs to honor your own sense of self and allow your own intuitive wisdom to guide you. You need to be the discerning guide within yourself and work in harmony with your own personal sense of healing. We all learn from teachers that come along throughout our lives, but they are not our masters unless we allow them to master over us. True learning is about listening to ourselves and mastering our own lives.

My intent is never to participate in the ongoing and escalating battles about Reiki and intuition. Reiki is unconditional. People are usually not unconditional. Rules have been generated by teachers to fit their own needs and wants, or even to help them through their own personal fears. I have poured over many Reiki books and noticed that no two agree. There are versions upon versions of treatment protocols, symbols, attunements, fees and yes, even rules.

Reiki Rules

In Frank Arjava Petter's book, *Reiki Fire* and in *The Original Reiki Handbook of Dr. Mikao Usui* by Christine M. Grimm, Petter explains how in 1997, T. Oishi gave him Usui's original handbook of notes and other old documents. These two books give details from Usui himself for such things as his hand placements on the recipient. Mikao Usui did not seem to have any rules. Petter states, "Intuitive Reiki by Dr. Usui is different: It asks that we free ourselves of the rules. Rules are meant to give us support. The moment that they begin to hinder us, they no longer fulfill their purpose." Petter went on to say, "We are all basically intuitive. We just have to learn to listen to the inspiration that is already there and 'translate' it correctly."

The myriad of Reiki books can be experienced as a rich variety of information celebrating diversity or as conflict. Reiki is alive within itself, and what is alive always changes and transforms. Reiki has already swept through the world. It seems that everyone is or at least knows a Reiki practitioner. What people do not expect is that Reiki is quite real. It is a distinct and powerful frequency of energy that heals the practitioner just as much as the client. The reality is that these changes are inevitable, expansive, positive, transformational . . . and sometimes extremely scary.

My Hopes for You

I want you to know that you are not alone as a Reiki person, you are not alone as an intuitive, and you are not alone as an intuitive Reiki practitioner. If your goal for being a Reiki person is to crank up your intuition, then you are on the wrong track. Reiki is not about developing your intuition. Your intuition being blasted open is simply a natural side effect of your internal healing. Reiki is all about opening up a certain energetic channel to be a vessel of cosmic love and Light for all. The act of opening such a channel also opens your intuitive pathways to receive non-physical information.

I will share some of my stories, but I have also reached out to other Reiki people to share their life stories with you. You will see yourself in some of our stories and potentially learn some new ideas that will assist you to expand beyond any limitations that hinder you.

I have three hopes for you as you read our stories:

Hope One: That you realize you are not alone in having intuitive experiences while giving Reiki to others or to yourself.

Hope Two: That you relax while reading this book so that you can open up even more to the blessed non-physical reality that exists.

Hope Three: That you deeply and beautifully explore your own body, thoughts, and energy field so you can know the depth of your own personal intuitive Reiki story and journal it here within this book without fear.

Personal Story: Tammy Barton

In being a licensed massage therapist for ten years, I had heard about Reiki from many of my fellow massage therapists, friends, and clients. Many were telling me I needed to learn Reiki and integrate the modality into my healing work.

I was definitely interested in learning Reiki but was also being patient in finding the perfect class and teacher. I wanted Reiki Levels I and II to not be taught within the same weekend. The Universe led me to the right teacher, and I found the blend of learning both Western and Eastern principles provided a wonderful balance and having the classes spread out over a few weeks gave me the opportunity to practice and become more confident in working with the healing powers and energies of Reiki.

What was really fascinating was learning about the Western principles being more structured with certain hand positions placed on different areas of the body, and the Eastern principles being more intuitive and scanning the physical and energetic body with the hands and eyes and trusting the intuitive hits on listening to the clients' body, mind, and spirit on where to go for the greatest level of healing.

The blend of the two principles made perfect sense to me because there are clients needing more structure and ones needing the intuitive flow of healing, and even both healing principles within the same healing session. In integrating Reiki with my clients, I have had the opportunity of witnessing beautiful healing transformations with the decreasing and diminishing of pain, stress, anxiety, and releasing old emotional wounds and increasing joy, love, laughter, peace, and harmony.

Within my own life I have also integrated and received Reiki healing, especially during the time my father was making his transition with leukemia. In experiencing a myriad of feelings and emotions, and being a caretaker for him and my mom during that time, I received Reiki and integrated Reiki on myself using the Reiki symbols, hand positions, and various meditation techniques to help with my emotional and physical body and truly noticed a difference in being able to sleep better, stress levels, and emotional and physical healing.

Learning and working with Reiki energy and symbols and integrating the modality into my healing practice has been a tremendous gift and has made a wonderful difference in my own personal healing and within the lives of my family, friends, and clients.

Tammy Barton
www.AtTheHealingPlace.com
Tammy@AtTheHealingPlace.com

CHAPTER 2

Be the Best Reiki Vessel

My Personal Intuitive Reiki Story

My own Reiki story began around 1991 at a woman's festival in Bloomington, Indiana. My dear feminist friends decided we should all attend one of the workshops called Reiki, taught by someone named Diane Stein. It was packed with more than a hundred women. Diane explained what Reiki is and then said she was going to give an attunement to every person there if they wanted to receive it. As I recall, we all placed ourselves in a giant circle and closed our eyes as she instructed us. She began the attunements on the far side of the room from me. She whispered to herself and waved her arms around the first woman then stepped to the next and then the next. I know this because I was peeking! I needed to see what on earth was happening. After the first twenty or so I decided there was no way this woman could attend to all these people, and yet she continued to give the attunements.

I grew up in a very dysfunctional family with a brutally sadistic mother, but intuition was an integral part of our life. We were all expected to use our intuition, though no one called it that. My family just shared experiences of seeing people in spirit, like who came to see them and what they had to say when they popped in. It was completely matter-of-fact information. No big deal at all.

It was not until I received my first Reiki attunement that new intuitive doors were flung open. I could not get those Reiki thoughts out of my everyday life. So I began to offer Reiki to people I knew. I asked them to spread the word about Reiki sessions, how they benefited from it, and what they noticed about themselves during the session. Little did they know that I was receiving all kinds of intuitive information about them during the sessions.

Each Reiki session began as massive waves of love pouring into me, filling me up, and then gushing through me and into the client's body. I then began to notice that in my mind's eye I was sometimes seeing colors or the lack of color when my hands were on the client's body. I looked for meaning behind the colors and the location of the colors, and I noticed that the lack of color was in direct correlation with their illness or disease. (The meaning of color is discussed more in Chapter 12.) Soon I was looking into the individual's physical body like an X-ray machine. I was fascinated and then I was hooked. Even in an openly intuitive family upbringing, no one mentioned that we could perceive the aura or look into a physical body.

I struggled and struggled some more before taking the next step. I was afraid, like you might be now. I wanted to share my intuitive awareness with my Reiki clients but was terrified that the information I was getting would then terrify them. Then the entire room would be filled with terror! I am laughing right now as I write these words to you.

No one became afraid—not one single person. I began first by asking them at the end of the Reiki session if they would like to hear about the intuitive information I received about them. Their eyes opened wide as they quickly said, "Yes! Of course I would." I asked them to sit down and I shared whatever I noticed. I did not try to interpret the awareness. I just described in detail what I noticed and asked if it made any sense to them. People's mouths hung open; they were stunned. Every one of them told me in different words how important and helpful this part of the Reiki was for them. They immediately became very open about their experiences while receiving Reiki. They also shared that they had wanted to tell me about similar experiences but had been afraid I would think they were too weird.

Do you understand that finally sharing my intuitive awareness allowed many others to realize their own intuitive knowledge, which in turn allowed them to open up and share? They did not go home and keep this a secret. My intuitive Reiki practice quickly grew as everyone's fear faded away.

Now many people would say that I am not even a Reiki practitioner because I no longer teach Reiki or offer sessions. Looking at my life from a distance, I guess it does look that way. I have been offering intuitive and medical intuitive readings for many years now. I teach my workshop "Become a Medical Intuitive: Seeing with X-Ray Eyes" all around the globe, and I specialize in teaching people how to do medical intuition with precision and accuracy.

No, I no longer offer Reiki sessions, but like every single one of us, I emanate Reiki in all that I do with others. If you allow Reiki into your life and embrace it into your heart and soul, you are emanating Reiki energy into every moment. We radiate Reiki no matter what we are doing with others.

I hope to prepare all Reiki practitioners at all levels through my Reiki books. I want to explain and to assure practitioners that, because of Reiki, positive changes are happening and will continue to happen in their personal lives. I hope to guide you through your own personal healing challenges and through your startling, unforeseen intuitive skills exploding into other realms of consciousness.

Reiki is alive and follows universal rules, not human rules. It is life force in action. It is constant and continues forever. It is a distinct and powerful frequency of energy that heals the practitioner just as much as the client. The attunement enters into your electromagnetic field, then your physical body, and then it radiates outward into your life, your awareness, your choices, and values. I want this book to assist you in understanding what is happening in your life and how to nurture the changes with confidence and love.

What leaps into your mind as you read this first portion of the book? What are your struggles regarding Reiki and intuition? Write down the instant details in your awareness.

_____

_____

_____

_____

_____

_____

_____

_____

_____

_____

_____

The Power of Thoughts

Your body, the earth, the Universe, and beyond are all part of the sea of living energy. The energy of the Universe is dynamic, expanding, and encompassing. Energy must always move, change, and transform. This is the natural temperament of energy. Everything around us, no matter the density of the object, has an electrical vibration, and everything pulsates at different frequencies. Your body is an electrically alive, vibratory being. Your body and the chair you are sitting on are both made of moving electrical particles, and yet you, as a human, are so different from that chair. One way we are different from the chair is that the energy of our physical body fluctuates under different circumstances. As different circumstances happen in our lives, we have thoughts about those experiences, and thoughts always lead to some type of feelings and emotions.

Science has discovered that energy follows human thought, and human thought tends to linger in locations toward which it is directed. Do you have any idea how profound and powerful that is in so many ways? Some energy healers already understand this concept, but to have science declare it to the public world is a giant step for mankind.

Our thoughts are profoundly powerful. Each thought emits a vigorous electrical signal that waves through our body and then emanates out into the world. Each sentence, which starts as a thought, is made of a series of words, and that string of words combines to form a precise vibration. Each thought and its subsequent emotion carries an energetic vibration, and that vibration is information and a message. Those energetic electrical messages surge through our body and rush out into the external world around us. Because we are thinking beings, the world around us responds to our thoughts. Because our thoughts are real things with substance, we are more powerful than we can ever imagine.

After that tiny introduction to the power of our thinking, let's talk about our emotions. Each emotion vibrates at its own frequency. Shame, guilt, fear, depression, and grief have slow, thick, sluggish, dense vibratory pulsations, while joy and love vibrate at faster, higher, and finer levels of electrical pulsations. The traits of shame, guilt, fear, and depression tend to become physical more quickly than other emotions. This sluggish, dense emotional energy tends to congregate in certain areas of the human body, causing an illness or a disease.

Dr. Joe Dispenza states in his book *Becoming Supernatural*, "For the most part your brain is a product of the past. It has been shaped and molded to become a living record of everything you have learned and experienced up to this point in your life . . . Experiences not only enhance the brain circuitry, but they also create emotions . . . Think of emotions as energy in motion . . . The frequencies of creative, elevated emotions like love, joy and gratitude are much higher than the emotions of stress, such as fear and anger, because they carry different levels of conscious intent and energy." He goes on to say, "The only way to change our lives is to change our energy . . . In other words, to change our state of being, we have to change how we think and how we feel."

YOUR MOMENT OF

Self-Awareness

Be honest with yourself and notice the theme of most of your thoughts and your emotions. Are you primarily a positive thinker and feeler or more of a negative one? Where do your thoughts and emotions congregate in your body? Write down the instant details in your awareness.

Thought, Emotion, and Body

Your head and your body are one unit. What happens in your head happens in your body. Most so-called advanced cultures focus on the use of our brain and ability to think but rarely identify that our brains actually sit on top of a physical body. Many of today's cultures around the world pay little attention to the body because there is such a strong focus on mental achievements such as awards, degrees, honors, and other accolades. In most societies, we might as well just be heads floating around life. We have lost track that we are a brain, mind, and a body.

Yes, your head and your body are one electrically alive unit. What happens in our brain and our thoughts also happens in our body. It is one complete and very intricately connected unit! The best example of thoughts affecting the body that I can think of—and that everyone can probably connect with—is worry. When you have a worry type of thought, your body thinks that the thing that you are worried about has just happened. Now take that concept to the next step. Let's say that you had that one particular worry ten times today. Your body thinks that the worry scenario actually happened ten times in twenty-four hours! So your body just took an emotional hit ten times for something that still has yet to happen.

The body and its interpretation of what is going on is very literal. Let's take one more step with the worry example. The worry thought has some type of emotion connected to it. Those particular emotions are often negative. Fear is a good example of an emotion that is part of a worried thought. Our physical body takes hit after hit because of our worries, and each worry creates another wave of fear. As worry thoughts repeat, the emotion of fear repeats, and the body takes another hit every time.

Now let's look at the positive healthy side of this story. Guided imagery, affirmations, deliberate positive thinking, and even thinking in commanding ways, work in the same manner. Deliberate positive thinking also creates electrical vibrations within our body. Positive thinking creates positive emotions that bring our physical bodies into positive healing and health. Taking charge and creating something positive in our body will make dramatic adjustments in the life energy that flows through us.

Take control of your thoughts for they are the generators of your emotions. Your emotions help you towards illness or lead you to wellness. Your thoughts and emotions can create a profound Reiki provider in you. Be the commander of you. Controlling and being in charge of your thinking mind is one of the keys to being the best vessel for Reiki!

YOUR MOMENT OF

Self-Awareness

Notice your body, brain, and your mind right now. How are you aware of being one unit and how are you not one unit? How are you in charge of your thoughts? How and when are you not in command? Write down the instant details in your awareness.

_____

_____

_____

_____

_____

_____

_____

_____

_____

_____

Patterns and Ruts

Have you noticed that it is very difficult to change the way you do things? For example, many of us have a certain pattern that we follow when we wake up—a morning routine. First you feed the cats their canned food, then you make your coffee, then, and only then, you take the next step. Some of us drive the exact same way to work each day when really there are a few different roads that lead to the same destination. Do you find yourself cooking the same meals week after week?

I believe that routine gives us a sense of stability. Maybe it gives us a reprieve from constantly needing to think in this busy, busy world. But it also leads us into a type of mind-numbing trance that creates mediocrity in our lives. By now you might be thinking, "What does Reiki have to do with this?"

At their invitation, I agreed to meet with two Reiki practitioners who wanted to give and to receive Reiki among the three of us. When we met they began asking me questions about Reiki and how I do it in particular. They had also attended some of my Reiki lectures where I taught about creating a sacred space for the giver but especially for the receiver.

Though I was a provider of Reiki, I had not taken the opportunity to receive it for a very long time. I was the last person to receive that day. I was so excited as I stretched out on the table. I was finally going to receive a very special and sacred Reiki session from two well-known providers. Each stood opposite the other, on either side of me. With my thoughts, I guided my energy to open and to be the receiver of blessed Reiki! They placed their hands on me, I took a deep breath—and they immediately began talking across me as if I was not there. They made the following comments:

"This is where I always place my hands on my clients."

"Where should we go to lunch when we are done?"

"Gosh, I don't know. Where do you want to go?"

"Well, we could get Mexican or Chinese."

"I always use this pattern of hand positions."

"This is the way that I always finish my Reiki sessions."

Many things were happening in this moment, but let me identify a few issues with the session:

1. Their thoughts were not focused on being the best vessel for Reiki healing.

2. They were not energetically creating an environment of healing, nor were they creating a sacred healing space for the receiver to experience healing. In fact, nothing sacred or healing was going on.

3. I felt like an object. They did not attend to me in the way that I did for them.

4. Reiki had become a pattern, a rut, and even boring for both of them.

5. There was no connection with the receiver on the table. They lost the sacredness of a Reiki session.

Ruts are often comfortable, but these same ruts also block us from the powerful, deliberate ability to create. Getting stuck in a pattern binds and squelches the physical flow of Reiki vibrations. Ruts are numbing and block out the intuitive information that is constantly trying to get through to us. Listen, read, or watch the techniques and methods in this book and also notice the positive techniques of others, and get out of your mind-numbing ruts regarding Reiki.

To me this is an ethical issue. Make sure that you are with your client 100 percent. I am not mentally listing my day's schedule or worrying about getting those restaurant reservations or wondering if my favorite store will have another sale. During a session with someone, I am right there for that particular person at that particular time. It is a sacred time and a sacred space and a sacred healing. Even in a quiet room, I repeat their name over and over in my mind. Then I pause and allow the Reiki and intuition to surge through me and into the receiver. Repeating the person's name within your mind is like a gentle mantra focusing the energy toward the client to strengthen the connection.

Excel as a clear vessel of Reiki for the person you are attending to. Really be present with them and for them. Instead of slipping into a rut, try something new. Open your awareness to the non-physical realm of healing. Notice the subtle shifts of coolness to warmth, or the images and sensations that flow into your mind as you enter into another person's life field. Be aware of colors changing in your mind's eye. Notice thoughts leaping out of nowhere. Feel the presence of a spirit guide. You will never be bored or in a rut again! When we take one step out of our rut, the view is new and often better. Our lives will excel as our Reiki excels. Step out of your own way and turn the healing back over to Spirit. You will again be fascinated and awestruck with the magic of Reiki.

YOUR MOMENT OF

Self-Awareness

Your life is created by every single thought you think. Are you in charge of your thoughts and emotions? If not, who is in charge of you? Where are your Reiki ruts? Write down the instant details in your awareness.

_____

_____

_____

_____

_____

_____

_____

Seven Important Concepts About Your Thoughts and Body

First concept: Accept diversity! Critical or judgmental thoughts and their subsequent emotions produce a constriction of the energy within your body. Expand your energy today by first accepting yourself as a unique human being who is continually learning and loving more and more. The more you accept yourself unconditionally, the more you will be able to accept others. Reiki embraces our diversity without judgment or criticism. Are you doing the same?

Second concept: You are naturally wired to be a vessel for Reiki. The more you utilize Reiki, the more easily your body adjusts to its surging frequency. Heavy or negative thoughts and emotions create areas of physical density in your body. The loving frequency of Reiki breaks up and disperses these restrictions and amplifies your ability to become a vital energy vessel for healing yourself and healing others.

We cannot improve on Reiki. It is the life force of the Universe—how could we possibly improve on that! As physical human beings, however, we can offer ourselves as an enhanced vessel for Reiki. We cannot improve upon the healing energy of Reiki, but what we can do is to constantly improve ourselves to be the best healing tool for Reiki and the people who need it.

Third concept: You are learning, not failing. We humans are profoundly creative in coming up with ways to convince ourselves that we are failures and inferior to everyone around us. Over the years, Reiki people have come to me for intuitive mentoring. Time after time when I ask people to recall the experiences they had during any of the attunements, they say things like the following: "I did not see anything or feel anything. Well, okay, maybe I noticed the warm hands of the teacher." Some were convinced that nothing happened and that "Reiki isn't really a thing. It is just hocus pocus." The sad response I hear most from people is, "There must be something wrong with me. I didn't notice anything, so I must not be right for Reiki and I cannot be a healer." People are so hard on themselves and so ready to dismiss their energetic abilities. I beg of you to allow yourself to be a student of intuitive Reiki. You are not failing—you are learning.

Fourth concept: Our thoughts create our lives. We attract into our life that which we love, that which we fear, and that which we think about and focus on. This is the law of attraction at work. The Universe cannot do otherwise. This is a physical and mechanical system that cannot be altered. Free yourself, your life, and your work by taking charge of your thoughts, emotions, and the vibrational energy signature you are emitting. Allow clients to come to you by seeing them in your mind and feeling them come through your door. Imagine drawing them to you like a magnet pulling pieces of metal to it. There are enough clients for everyone to thrive. The right ones will be drawn to you. They will be the ones that you can help.

Science has discovered that energy follows human thought—in other words, thoughts are energy! Scientists are stating that the human brain and mind is dynamic, creative, and in charge! They have found that our thoughts can influence our environment, move objects, and make a difference in our world.

Fifth concept: Create a sacred space with your thoughts. There are specific ways to improve our role in the healing process. It is up to the healer to create a sacred space for a session by creating a spiritual ambiance in a room or space for healing. But much more important is to Reiki that space. Sending healing into the room will cleanse it of emotions and density. You can power up the space with the Cho Ku Rei, for instance. Science has not only discovered that energy follows thought, but also energy lingers within an area. Send Reiki into the space before the recipient arrives for a session. They will feel it.

Do not chatter during the session unless responding to the client. I actually inform my client that I do not talk during the session unless responding to a comment made by the client. I explain that my silence helps me to stay in a sacred space to be the clearest vessel for Reiki. I also explain that I am at my best when I am quiet. Remember the practitioners talking about where to go to lunch while they were supposed to be a focused channel for me? When you think about the word "sacred," feel an emotion about being sacred and also ask your spirit guides for sacredness to happen. It is just as simple as that because our thoughts and emotions create our reality.

Sixth concept: Create powerful intent with focused thought. What does intent really mean, and what is it in a Reiki session? The word "intent" basically means focused thought. Your ability to focus your thoughts empowers your intent to be that clear, open, flowing river for Reiki. There should be no effort or sense of working hard. If it feels that you are working hard, then you are getting in the way of Reiki and healing. Your focused intent is to simply be present for the person who has come to you for help. Do not think about the errands you need to do when this person leaves. Do not remember that you are out of milk or you need to mow the grass. Stay in the room and with the person who needs you. Be present because you are a vital link in the healing system of Reiki. When we are the supervisor of our thoughts we are no longer victims of our emotions and subsequent reactions.

For another example of a focused intent, we might be asked by the Reiki guides to set a focused intent for a different purpose. Spirit guides may direct your intent to create a laser beam of Reiki energy and send it into a certain area of body that is ill. I have been guided to laser into a cancerous tumor or to seal something together, such as eye surgery when the retina has detached. This is an extremely delicate but powerful healing technique.

When I have received this laser beam guidance, the fingertips of one hand move together to form a point. An image of a fluorescent type of glowing light, about the size and width of a pencil, goes deep into the body and burns away the tumor or seals the broken bone or heals the situation in some manner that is guided by Spirit and not by me.

Seventh concept: How else can I improve? I often hear this question from students. "Is there anything else I can do to be a more powerful channel for Reiki?" My answer is the following. Besides deliberately directing your natural toroidal field, which is discussed in Chapter 5, there is one other simple way to enhance your personal energy flow on a daily basis.

We humans are, in general, terribly dehydrated. Make sure that you drink lots and lots of water. I do not mean increase fluids such as sodas, coffee, and tea. Our human bodies are mostly water, and they cannot function well when the water level is low. Coffee and teas are dehydrating to the human body.

We are electrical beings and Reiki is the electrical surge of a loving, living life force. Water is a superb avenue for electricity. For example, suppose an electrical line fell into a pool of water that collected on a street after a storm. We know to steer clear of that pool of water because the electrical wires touching the water mean the entire pool is electrified. The earth and our bodies are both approximately 70 percent water. That level of water allows us to function as natural channels for the electrical nature of Reiki and intuition.

Our bodies are also great vehicles for electricity. Our physical body requires water to conduct the electrical signals in our nervous system between brain, organs, muscles. If we are dehydrated, not only is the physical body affected, but the electrical nature of Reiki and intuitive wisdom is also inhibited. Drink a glass of water before, during, and after each Reiki session. You will feel the difference. Intuition and Reiki are optimized by a healer whose body is an open, flowing, water-based system. Breathing with awareness, drinking lots of water, and sensing the fullness of love will help you optimize the current of Reiki and intuitive information flowing through you.

YOUR MOMENT OF

Self-Awareness

What thoughts, sensations, and knowing do you have about yourself as you read each of the seven concepts? Notice without criticism. Could your thoughts, emotions, and body be improved and in what ways? How creative are you at convincing yourself you are a failure? Explore that now. How do you try to convince yourself that you cannot do Reiki, that you are not a healer and you are not intuitive? How excellent are you at convincing yourself you cannot do this? Write down the instant details in your awareness.

Please read each concept again. Write down the instant details of your awareness.

Concept One

_____

_____

_____

_____

_____

Concept Two

_____

_____

_____

_____

_____

Concept Three

_____

_____

_____

_____

_____

Concept Four

_____

_____

_____

_____

_____

Concept Five

Concept Six

Concept Seven

Personal Story: Heather McCutcheon

This is an excerpt from the book Connecting the Dots: from ad exec to
energy practitioner, *by Heather McCutcheon, Founder of the Reiki Brigade.*

Prior to doing this work, I believed, as many do, that a very small percentage of the population is psychic and the rest of us are not. Now I understand that there is a rapidly growing number of people who recognize that energy contains information they can interpret and who are working to hone this ability. Others have not yet recognized that they have this ability, and therefore have not begun to develop their energetic literacy.

Mary came in a few months after her mother's passing. She was grieving the loss and actively taking care of herself in a number of ways, including doing a juice cleanse and getting some energy work. When I began her clearing by working with her root chakra, she felt sensations and movement in her throat. I had come to understand that feeling sensations in one chakra while work was being done in another meant there was a glitch in communication between the two. I kept one hand over her first chakra and moved my other hand over her throat chakra to connect the two and improve the energy flow. While I knew nothing about this woman's family life other than the fact that she had lost her mother, I felt in my body and blurted out, "You need to talk to your dad about your mom!" When she heard this, she began to cry.

Apparently, Mary's mother was nurturing, emotionally available, and provided a source of gentle moral support and guidance for Mary. They had a close bond based on open and intimate communication. Mary's father was an alcoholic, neither in touch with his emotions nor prone to nurturing parenting. Now that her mother had passed, Mary was adjusting to the fact that her father was not going to be able to fill that role for her, and this void would be a significant part of her loss.

There were shifts taking place in the dynamics between her root chakra (survival via close community, of which parents are a big part) and her throat chakra (which governs communication and speaking your truth). I believe getting my hands into the energy between these two chakras put me right in the midst of the information flow, which came to me as an immediate download. This is an example of claircognizance through my sixth chakra. I had no time to process the information before it turned into words and I spoke them, an action of my throat chakra.

Jennifer came to my office after her husband was diagnosed with stage D pancreatitis due to alcoholism and had his pancreas removed. The prognosis was not good. He was very successful in the music industry, and they were in an enviable position both socially and financially.

She was distraught, as would be expected, and I thought we would be dealing with her grief and anxiety about the situation. Instead, I was drawn to her third eye. I felt a big electrical storm over her forehead and spent a lot of time clearing that out and recharging the chakra. She felt dopey after the session, which is common, and after re-acclimating to her body, she thanked me, paid my fee, and left.

She called me several days later to tell me that the night after her session she'd had an epiphany. She was cooking dinner and walked over to the couch to ask her husband a question. As she looked at him, she just knew that he was still drinking. She confronted him and found he had been stashing bottles around the house and sneaking drinks whenever he could. "How could I have missed the signs?" she said. It was all so obvious in retrospect.

The next time she came in, she told me she was also able to read between the lines in conversation, whereas before she took everything at face value. Sub-textual information was now more readily available. She attributed this to our work with her third eye.

As it had done for me, energy work was helping others to perceive the world with more accuracy, helping the blind to see.

Heather McCutcheon
www.ReikiBrigade.com
heather@reikibrigade.com

YOUR MOMENT OF

Self-Awareness

Take one minute to think thoughts of being in charge. Really feel the breath of life coming into your body. Allow yourself to think and feel Reiki and love. Let yourself, in reality, physically fill up with Reiki and love. Write down the instant details of your awareness.

_____

_____

_____

_____

_____

_____

_____

_____

_____

CHAPTER 3

Common Causes of Suffering

Some people schedule Reiki sessions out of curiosity, but most people are seeking relief from some type of suffering. Suffering can be mental, emotional, or physical. We humans have so many reasons and ways to suffer. There is a direct correlation between physical pain and emotional pain. Underneath physical pain, emotional pain is always buried deep within their being. The stronger or more overwhelming the physical pain, the more profound the underlying emotional pain is as well. Sometimes we are conscious of the source of our emotional pain, but usually we suppress it so deeply that we no longer know where it is coming from. Sorrow, distress, and anguish are never really suppressed or dormant. Everything is energy, even emotional pain, and it cannot remain locked away. It moves, shifts, and builds throughout the emotional body and then, eventually, it becomes more physical in nature, congregating in your physical body. These restricted areas begin on an energetic level resulting in a collapsing of the flow in that area. As the restriction continues over time, it also becomes physically denser and more solid.

The healer receives a great deal of information from the location where the symptoms manifest in the physical body. Different emotions tend to congeal and thicken, eventually leading to restricted areas of the body. For example, someone who has tremendous ongoing pain in their low back will have old emotional issues around security. Someone with chronic pain in their shoulders tends to carry the weight of responsibility for everyone with them. (For more detailed information regarding the body, mind, emotional connection, please see my book *Become a Medical Intuitive*.) Here are some of the least discussed causes of suffering.

Empaths

If you identify as an empath, I ask that you be open and consider what I am about to say. An empath accurately picks up and feels the emotions and suffering of people around him or her. Such emotional hyperawareness happens anywhere—while you are in the shopping center or at church or with your hobby group or watching the news on TV or in thousands of other situations. To be an empath means to absorb everyone's emotions happening around you and to make them your own. It is as if you are a dry sponge soaking up the pain of the world.

Empaths suffer much more than the individuals around them. They not only carry their own life struggles, but they take on the burdens of every suffering person that comes into their awareness. As a result, the painful energetic burdens of others collect within the empath's field and eventually within the physical body. Empaths cannot maintain their equilibrium or their own health because they take on the agony of so many others. If you recognize my description, then please take heed. If you keep absorbing the sorrows around you, you will not make it as a Reiki practitioner or as an intuitive Reiki practitioner. There is a strong potential that you will become more ill than any of the people around you.

Esther Hicks succinctly described taking on another's struggles as if they are your own in a workshop in San Diego, California, on February 15, 2003: "You cannot get sick enough to help people get better. You cannot get poor enough to help people thrive. It is only in your thriving that you have anything to offer anyone. If you're wanting to be of an advantage to others, be as tapped in, tuned in, and turned on as you can possibly be."

Instead of merging with the suffering of the world around you, I ask that you step back and become an interested observer of the world around you. Do not throw yourself into the center of the agony. Watch from a broader, less reactive view. Begin to understand that each person is on a personal mission to learn, develop, and expand through experiences. Some experiences are of pain, illness, and trauma, but also some are having experiences of wonderment and awe and everything in between. Observe without judgement. Observe without absorbing. A true healer does not merge with the ones who suffer. The true healer holds out the brightest, clearest loving Light for the suffering to find hope and the path to peace.

Personal Story: Lisa Rathore, RN

Reiki continues to teach me about faith and trust in the healing process and in myself as a Reiki practitioner. Besides practicing Reiki, I am a registered nurse. So how do I explain my use of Reiki in what I do? Well, it has to do with the concept of pain. I work in two seemingly disparate areas of nursing: emergency and psychiatric. In both settings, however, I have witnessed Reiki energy flowing in to mitigate pain of all types. Pain is an odd phenomenon that can sometimes be difficult to articulate by the one experiencing it. Physical pain may be observed and sensed objectively, but only sorely felt subjectively. Then, run the gamut of all other pain by various definitions. This is a shared human condition.

As a nurse, I strive to care for my patients in a manner of high standard. Yet there had been times that I'd felt lack in nursing intervention to alleviate a person's pain and discomfort, aside from medications, or standard care. This led to a feeling of "burnout" and frustration from time to time as health conditions become more complex to treat.

I soon discovered Reiki along the way and even Tina Zion encouraged me toward learning Reiki. It is a great healing tool for me, personally, and it has given me better perspective while doing my job. Of course, good judgment is paramount in discerning the context of when and how to appropriately use Reiki, so that respectful care may be given within the unique healthcare environment.

I like to allow space for that to happen and I have learned to do so by actively trusting my intuition. To maintain professional relationships, I use a "hands at a distance" approach, and I typically verbalize request for permission to use Reiki first. If not, I will silently ask. In my experience, beneficial effects from Reiki energy may or may not be acknowledged by patient or practitioner. It depends upon the situation and the patient. I've seen the healing work of Reiki on visceral pain related to a medical problem, physical withdrawal symptoms from an addiction, all the way to existential pain found on the mental/emotional, psychic, and spiritual levels.

My historic tendency towards impatience with sought after tangible outcomes has been gently replaced with a secure understanding and trust, as I continue to revel in how Reiki's versatility to comfort an emotional crisis easily extends to its supportive analgesic effects on procedural pain management.

Then there is that which we do not see. It has unfolded my higher awareness giving me the ability to "sense" its more subtle workings. I've let go of needing proof that it works because sometimes its healing outcome may not be so apparent. The adaptive, quality range that Reiki healing energy exemplifies is an organic, useful process that proves credence in its application of the profound and practical kind. Especially with the challenges many of us are faced with today.

I anticipate that Reiki therapy will integrate further along the progression of our healthcare needs, as I've found my patients accept it with ease. Most of them have a basic understanding of Reiki and realize that it is non-invasive and safe. Many have reported immediate benefit right after a healing session.

Through the practice of mindfulness as a key approach to allowing the energy flow of Reiki, I have personally broadened my awareness of how effectively Reiki works. It does increase one's intuition naturally. I'm of the belief that we are here to learn life lessons via the use of our free will and power of choice, even at the most sublime level. We may accept the benefits of Reiki healing energy for our highest good on any or all planes of existence. Reiki tends to go where it is accepted and needed most by the person receiving it.

I've learned that although one may not "see" it working right away, like prayer, sometimes it's the things we cannot see with our eyes, which may have the greatest effect on the healing process. This I say without judgment because Reiki is a universal energy, applicable to anyone who seeks its healing benefits.

I've had the opportunity to learn Reiki and experience deep calming peace with a reverent sense of balance, which I continue to practice. Reiki has allowed me the honor to be of service to others with this purpose in mind as I share it with those on their own healing journey.

Lisa Rathore, RN
Reikilove9@gmail.com

Personal Story: Rev. Dr. Michelle Walker, DNP

As an empathic child I could hear Spirit though I did not gain an understanding or the wisdom to listen to them until later in my adult years. I began laying on of hands instinctively as a child when an animal was present or someone was ill.

As an adult, that intuitive feeling of laying on of hands and my desire to help sick people drew me into a healing career of nursing. After a near-death experience ten years ago, I sustained multiple injuries resulting in many surgeries and chronic pain throughout my spine and extremities. Traditional medicine was not effective, which lead me to seek out alternative healing modalities. I tried chiropractic, physical therapy, acupuncture, massage, essential oils, but still experienced no long-standing relief. Then a colleague offered to give me a Reiki session, and my life changed.

That first session I immediately felt calmer and lighter, as if fifty pounds was left behind. I felt divine love and angelic fluffy energy all around that filled the room, and best of all my neck and back pain were gone. I rose from the massage table and proclaimed, "I must learn how to do this," and my journey through Reiki attunements began. With each level of attunement came physical and emotional shifts, which encouraged me to continue my spiritual awakening.

Due to the healing that was occurring with each Reiki session, I felt safe to allow my intuitive abilities to awaken. My clairsentience was the first to be enhanced. The first time and every time I performed Reiki, my hands and feet began to heat up, and I felt that heat surging in and out of my being. Though I always had sensitivity to temperatures in my hands, that sensitivity was dramatically heightened with the slightest shift in temperature or density after my first Reiki attunement. This still assists me as a healthcare provider assessing my patients during physical exams.

Next my clairvoyance began to reopen with each session, starting with various colors in and around the chakras and hotspots of the body. Then the colors began to turn into animals, shapes, dense areas, words, symbols, and eventually beings. These divine helpers were angels, guides, and loved ones offering their guidance and assistance in the healing. I began to interact with and ask these divine beings questions as I moved over the body during a session. I would gain more information such as what particular colors meant and what animals and symbols meant. This inquiry would lead me to be drawn to certain books or articles or people who could shed light on that topic. It became very serendipitous.

As I moved from one level of Reiki to another, learning about and experiencing each type of symbols and energies, I began to meet new like-minded souls on similar journeys. My training consisted of Usui, which gave me the foundation levels I, II and Master, then Seichim Sekhem I, II and Master, and finally completing Karuna I, II, Master. Each type of Reiki has subtle differences in their energetic signature, but all have a place when healing the complexities of body, mind, and spirit.

Over the next ten years, I had many teachers assist me in learning new skills—or relearning skills I knew in other times, however you choose to look at it. I also began to perceive my life and energy very differently. Learning that everything is energy and can be changed through intention and divine assistance created a different level of mindfulness that assisted me in more fully living the Reiki principles. I continue to provide Reiki along with other healing modalities to family, friends, pets, patients, and myself as the need arises. Reiki is still a part of my therapeutic regimen to maintain pain relief.

Rev. Dr. Michelle Walker, DNP
EmpoweredWellness.org
DrWalkerEmpoweredWellness@gmail.com

YOUR MOMENT OF

Self-Awareness

Have you identified yourself as an empath? Has being an empath led to an increase in your own emotional pain? Does it make sense to be the clearest Reiki Light for others rather than merging into the suffering of the world? Write down the instant details in your awareness.

Energy Drainers

Some people tend to drain everyone around them. These draining people are suffering too. It is common for people to unconsciously draw on the energy of everyone around them. They truly do not know that they can be the generators of their own essence and vitality. These people are emotionally damaged at a young age in their current life, or they have brought the damage with them from a past life. The earlier traumatic experiences have left them needy and, at some level, victimized. As a result, they unconsciously pull energy from people around them until those people cannot tolerate the vampire-like depletion any longer. The depleted person usually struggles and suffers from constant frequently being drained by others. They also struggle to identify why they cannot stand to be near the vampire-like individual.

Making Someone Else's Life More Important

As a mental health counselor, I noticed another cause of emotional pain. Some of my clients would intervene repeatedly in the life of a loved one, trying to help when their loved one considered it as unwelcomed interference. These clients would also state that they could not be happy until their loved one changed their life. My clients were seriously disturbed and even panic-stricken over their loved one mishandling their life. My clients were in real emotional pain due to their own personal beliefs about what another human's life should be like. They were so involved in wanting something for someone else that they were often unable to realize that they themselves were not making those same decisions in their own life. Because they were completely engrossed in their loved one's decisions, they had lost sight of their own life and its importance.

As your subtle intuitive awareness grows, you will witness the larger picture of life. You will become intensely aware that each individual, even your loved ones, are living in their own eternal soul development. Each individual's struggles and also their joys are part of their soul's potential mindfulness and their developing consciousness. From the greater viewpoint of intuitive wisdom, you can help each individual when you can and offer wisdom if and when it is asked for. More importantly, you will grasp an overview of the potential possibilities and choices that your loved one is learning about.

From this vantage point, you can stop being consumed by the ones you care about the most and get in charge of your own thoughts, emotions, and energy. Be the master of your thoughts, and your energy field will respond to the signals of each thought. The brightness of your light will always guide a loved one, or a client, much more than losing your happiness by getting sucked into their life choices. Be the brightest light in your own life and the brightest light for others.

Living By Someone Else's Rules

Over and over my client's will discover that they have been trying to live the way someone demands that they live. Someone else demands that my clients make the choices that they know will be the best for them. All the while my clients yearn to live to the beat of a different drummer. Every time my clients try to break free and live a life that is right for their own soul, guilt drives them back. The thoughts and emotions of guilt keep us held back, and such guilt will eventually create not only emotional pain but physical pain as well.

Personal Story: Jenny Chen

I grew up in a temple and was taught about having compassion and unconditional love for others. I met my ex-husband and his mother at the temple where I grew up. They both were spiritual teachers at the temple. I used to put them on a pedestal and looked up to them. I believed they were very spiritual people and lived their lives in accordance with the holy teachings. When we got married, I truly looked forward to spiritual growth with them.

However, since the day after our wedding, they turned out to be completely different from whom I have known. They laid down rules that I had to obey including being distanced from my parents and my close friends because they were in a lower class than us (my ex-husband and his family). My thoughts and behavior were too worldly and far from spirituality. They had to discipline me, including beating me up. Whenever I had different opinions from them, he would be so angry to the point that he would destroy anything in front of him and his fists would be like rainfalls on my head. His fists wouldn't stop until I apologized to him and also had to explain to him how I was wrong. In the beginning, I wouldn't know what to explain because I had no idea how I was wrong. Slowly I learned to tell him what he would be happy to hear. It first created tremendous conflicts within me because what they told me was so different from what I had learned about spirituality. But my perception of them being very spiritual made me choose to believe them. I would question my own belief in spirituality. Eventually, I slowly was brainwashed and lost my own identity. Every day, I lived on my tiptoes and hoped not to trigger their anger. All I wished was having a quiet day. Future was complete dark to me. I lived like a puppet on a string in their hands.

One day at my ex-husband's work conference, I met a medical director. He insisted on teaching me Reiki. I was not interested at all. My ex-husband really wanted me to take the Reiki class so he could establish a connection with this medical director because he was in a higher professional position than him. Hence, I took Reiki I and II from this medical director on a one-on-one sitting.

Something magical happened afterward. It was almost like a light switched on in my head. It swiped away my confusion and allowed me to see the abusiveness of my marriage.

It somehow also gave me the courage and wisdom to handle unreasonable requests from my ex-husband and his mother. My marriage situation consequently improved, and the chaotic moments significantly lessened. I also started seeing a therapist secretively to heal myself from these years of mental abuse. With the professional help in addition to Reiki, I started gaining mental strength slowly. I started to think about how to improve my marriage situation.

In the following year, that medical director highly recommended me taking Reiki III and advanced Reiki training with his teacher who is a spiritual energy healer. With the further training on advanced Reiki, my intuition had developed significantly. During one of our sessions, I realized the Karmic past-life relationship between me, my ex-husband, and his mother. It allowed me to forgive them for whatever happened in our current marriage.

Our marriage ended at the end of our third year. I came out of it much stronger and wiser. It also helped me to be a more intuitive and compassionate healer today. For all of that, I have to thank Reiki and the medical director who taught me Reiki in the first place. Last year when I met him again, I found out that he actually knew my situation at that time intuitively when he first met me. He was hoping Reiki could help me, and it really did.

Jenny Chen
http://www.serenelylove.com

Five Steps to Stop Emotional Pain

1. Begin thinking and knowing that you are no longer losing your life or being victimized.

2. Imagine and feel like you are now in charge of you. Command your energy to reject and repel any attempts to be drained or consumed.

3. Speak to your body using commanding thoughts. Direct it to pull out any draining connections that are negatively affecting you and give them back to the one who is draining you. Send a strong energetic message: "No. I reject and repel all the negative parts of life from that person or situation. I keep all positive energy and qualities of this person."

   Note: This will not end a relationship. You are energetically remaining connected to the most positive part of that individual.

4. Ask Reiki to fill you up with the unconditional love of Reiki. Send Reiki to the relationship with the intent of cleansing all negativity. Then send Reiki to power up the positive in the relationship.

5. If at all possible, teach people that you have learned a new energy technique. Show them how to build up their own energy field by thinking more positive thoughts, which lead to positive emotions, which lead to healing the body. Be the confident

leader to teach others just how powerful they are. You are not drained by them any longer. Be the light for those who are struggling around you. You are the illumination in your own life and can be the illumination in the lives of many, many others.

Use everything as an experience of learning something about yourself. You must reach the viewpoint of allowing a sense of learning about yourself in every situation. Use every single event and every single moment in your life as a time to learn more about yourself and to expand more into a spiritual level of awareness to see the greater picture of life and your part and position in the world around you.

YOUR MOMENT OF

Self-Awareness

What thoughts and emotions are you personally having now? Be aware of the thoughts and emotions that keep popping up, or the ones you ruminate about. Notice shame, guilt, or self-blame. A great deal of our suffering comes from holding onto these kinds of emotions. Are you blaming yourself for something—or everything? Emotions like blame carry an extremely low energy vibration, and you add that energy to whatever your current situation is. Write down the instant details of your awareness.

What do you know about your own suffering? Has it lead you to anything positive in your life? What might you learn from your personal or private suffering? Can you stop merging into the suffering around you and be luminous for all? Write down the instant details of your awareness.

CHAPTER 4

Overcoming Fear with Love

Fear

Are you willing to explore your possible fears about intuition and your intuitive abilities?

You are energy, a matrix of energy, an aura, and then a physical body. I cannot say it enough—thoughts, emotions, and the body are powerful, connected energetic currents. Thoughts and emotions that repeat over and over will tend to remain in the human energy field. The longer we have negative thoughts and fearful emotions, the denser our energy becomes. That thickened energy usually begins to manifest at a physical level in the physical body.

Fear constricts and chokes the flow of all energy. Fear chokes the flow of Reiki and strangles the flow of intuitive wisdom. You will not be able to perceive crucial information about your client's struggles, illness, and disease if you are in any degree of fear.

As I travel the world teaching medical intuition, I always find a large portion of the students have received at least the first level of Reiki. It is so amazing to see that Reiki is alive and active all over the world. Reiki people come to my workshops because they know something is happening during the Reiki sessions they are giving. They know that sometimes they are perceiving strange visions, feelings, smells, sounds, messages, spirit interactions, and even more.

Most students who come to my workshop want to understand what is happening. They want to open up this ability and receive even more intuitive information than what they are currently getting. And yet others are afraid. They do not know if they want to encourage the intuitive information they are receiving or if they want to shut it down. Reiki people in general keep telling me that they need help and want guidance to understand what is happening. Fear is constricting and hinders the flow of Reiki, and it also limits intuition. In the self-awareness moment below, you can read a list of the fears and worries that I hear about in every workshop, no matter where in the world I am.

YOUR MOMENT OF

Self-Awareness

To understand yourself more deeply, allow yourself to acknowledge your fear and worries. Read each fear or worry and consider if or how it applies to you. Write down the instant details of your awareness.

I am worried or afraid of . . .

seeing spirits _____

being overwhelmed _____

doing harm _____

the unknown _____

change _____

failure _____

being wrong _____

just making it all up _____

not being worthy to help others _____

not being worthy of receiving intuitive wisdom _____

the unknown spirit world dominating me _____

loving the spirit world so much, I might want to die _____

family / friends knowing I do this work _____

going against my family's religion _____

not being normal _____

knowing about someone's death _____

You may have a different fear than you see on this list. If you do not see the fear or worry that you struggle with, then write it here.

_____

_____

_____

_____

_____

_____

To be an excellent Reiki person, it is essential that you make yourself aware of your fears and worries. It is even more essential as an intuitive Reiki person to be aware of those fears and worries and to catch yourself the second fear rushes into your thoughts. When it rushes into your mind, it is also rushing throughout your body.

It seems that the power of Reiki generates strong feelings within people. You will see fear of Reiki and intuition in the most surprising people and in the most surprising places. For example, you may have dear friends who suddenly become fearful because you are going to take a Reiki class or do a Reiki share. Your family may demand that you never speak about it at family gatherings. Even people with whom you have always felt a deep and private trust may suddenly be afraid to be around you. You may feel crushed and shocked by their comments because you love and adore these people and you love and adore Reiki. Hopefully, you will then hear the soft words of Spirit in your mind: "You can never do harm with Reiki." Listen to the truth of your intuition and the unconditional love within yourself. If you yearn to learn about Reiki and if you yearn to give Reiki to others, please trust yourself.

Personal Story: Tina M. Horton, CMT

I began using Reiki energy therapy around 2005. I was beginning my education for massage therapy at a local community college and was taking an elective class as part of my second semester called Human Energies. The class was about energy work—how to find it, feel it, work with it, and use it. The modality was called Healing Touch, and I was what the teacher called a "natural." During the sixteen-week course, the teacher mentioned Reiki energy therapy as a compliment to the work we were doing. I took it upon myself to find out more, and within six months was attuned to level I and level II. Since then I have used Reiki on a daily basis, both on myself and clients that are willing to receive. Three years later I finally took the Master/Teacher level at a local metaphysical shop. Three years ago, I began to teach Reiki energy therapy at the same shop where I learned my Master/Teacher certification.

Reiki Energy has taught me so many lessons over the last decade that to list them would take the rest of the day. The lessons have been as simple as the energy is there and all I have to do is trust it and it will go where it needs to go and do what it needs to do. It has been as complicated as learning to trust myself. I have learned every single day from the energy. Lessons that have helped me be a stronger facilitator of healing. I have added other energy therapies to my "tool bag" over the years, but it all started with Reiki. I want to share with you the three biggest lessons I have learned from the energy.

1. Your intent is the single most important thing you have. It really does guide the energy! It really is everything. You will hear it a thousand times, it will become part of your practice.

2. Anyone—yes, *anyone*—can do Reiki! Provided you do not have a mental/physical/or emotional blockage, anyone can learn to harness Reiki energy and use it.

3. Stay humble! I have learned I am not the healer—that speaks of my ego and ego has no place in the healing arts. I am the facilitator; I listen to the energy and follow its lead. It knows where to go and how to get there. My job is to guide it only and support the healing process. The energy knows more than I will ever comprehend, so I trust it!

The lesson that will challenge you the most will be to trust yourself. You cannot do this wrong. If you go through the proper classes, you work with it every day, and you trust yourself, you will grow in ways you never thought possible.

Tina M. Horton, CMT
tinahorton.ps@gmail.com
(260) 908-0976

YOUR MOMENT OF

Self-Awareness

This is also a moment of honesty within yourself about yourself. How have your fears and worries gotten in your way? When has it happened, and how will you catch yourself so you can get more in charge of you and alter your thoughts to trust? What will it take to trust your own wisdom? What will it take to trust the intuitive wisdom that comes to you? Write down the instant details of your awareness.

_____

_____

_____

_____

_____

_____

_____

_____

I, myself, absolutely trust whatever leaps into my awareness no matter what it is or how strange it is. The key is to trust the pop or the leap. If an awareness pops in, I trust it. The second I decided to trust the pop no matter what, my intuitive awareness blossomed wide open and my accuracy surpassed anything I could have ever imagined.

Love

For just a moment, remember a time when you felt deep, profound, unbelievable *love*.

Remember the physical waves of sensations in your body. It could have been the first time that you looked out across the ocean or looked into the eyes of a baby or saw the person you were meant to be with forever. It could be a memory of your lover's touch or a family member sharing a special moment. Remember the waves of energy that filled your chest with warmth and fullness. Your thoughts were not so prominent because, in that moment, swift, delicate, electrical wave frequencies called love flashed through the core of your essence. You experienced the lightest, finest electrical frequency that is possible for human beings. If only for a flash of a moment, all of life is gentle, caring, and benevolent. At that moment, it is difficult to believe that you could ever feel less than love ever again.

Before I begin a Reiki session I recall that sensation of love and I do my best to just remember and allow that feeling to come forward and through me. Even if I have never laid eyes on the client, I fill myself up with those electrically alive waves of love. Then I send that electrical frequency of absolute, unconditional love deep within their physical body. That is true Reiki, and true Reiki is without criticism, judgment, or conditions.

In *The Original Reiki Handbook of Dr. Mikao Usui*, the author states, "It is simple to carry out the Reiji ritual (indication of the Reiki power) in a mechanical way, but that isn't the point of it. Try to get involved with your whole heart each time you do it, just like the very first time. The most important components involved in this are love and attention. These two qualities will show your client and you the path to healing and well-being."

So before your client walks into your Reiki room, take a moment to remember a time in your life when you felt what I call "ooey gooey" love—when love was that physical sensation washing through you. Reiki is that warm, full rush of love. That is what you send into your client. That is what flows through you no matter what you might think of them personally . . . no criticism, no judgement, no negative thoughts. This is what unconditional love is. It means no negative thoughts of criticism or judgement are involved. No matter who walks into your office—no matter what they look like, no matter how they are dressed or what hair style they have, no matter how much they weigh or how dirty they are, no matter what else is going on—you fill up with this vibrational current of Reiki love, and that is what you send into every single person.

Here is a different kind of love story. My dear friend was diagnosed with uterine cancer, stage 2, and was scheduled for surgery in three weeks. She asked me to give Reiki to her, which I did each week prior to surgery. Just as I was finishing her first session, an intuitive thought leaped into my mind. *Tell her to place her hands on her abdomen for a few minutes three times every day and send love deep into her uterus.* I told my friend exactly what just flashed into my mind.

She responded, "How do I do that?"

I replied, "Begin by remembering a time when love was a physical sensation floating through you. You suddenly sensed your heart inside your chest feel full and rich, or goose bumps rushed across your skin as you held a new baby in your arms, or you saw the ocean for the first time and felt the water softly misting your face. Can you remember a time when love just gushed through you? When you recall your own personal moment, your body will give you physical sensations of the energetic vibrations of love. Feel pure love, then send that frequency into your body."

Then my friend said, "Should I cancel my surgery?"

"Absolutely not!" I said. "Please do not cancel the surgery, but do your homework assignment every day, and even do it the morning of the surgery."

Not only did she do well through the surgery, but the lab report after the surgery found only a stage 1 level of cancer. The surgeon stated that he could not explain why the tumor was less than half the size that it appeared on the CAT scan. This was a dramatic improvement in three weeks. Reiki and deeply loving herself unconditionally three times a day for only a few moments physically altered the cancer. My friend was not "fighting against" the cancer as most people do. She was loving the uterine cancer away.

Love without any preconditions or requirements has the highest, finest, lightest healing vibration of all. Love cannot be contained and it has no boundaries. We are meant to love others and we are meant to love ourselves. Can you imagine right now being so proud of yourself for being who you are meant to be? Can you imagine emanating love to everyone no matter what?

Allow love to softly emerge from your heart and flood your entire body, all of your thoughts, and your entire energy field. We are each capable of allowing and creating this all-encompassing electrical charge within ourselves first. Love unconditionally, no matter what is happening and no matter who is involved and no matter how the other person is acting. This is true Reiki.

YOUR MOMENT OF

Self-Awareness

Remember your precious moments of love. Practice getting in charge of your mind and your energy and create that flow of love now. Can you love someone that much right now? Can you love and cherish yourself that much now as well? Can you love everyone at this same level without judgement right now? Create it and describe it here. Write down the instant details of your awareness.

CHAPTER 5

Your Daily Energy Shower—It Is Vital

Most of us take a shower or bath daily to keep the physical portion of ourselves clean. It is even more important to cleanse our energy field. It is up to us to keep our energy body robust, resilient, sparkling bright, and with no weakened areas. It is important that we deliberately keep our field at its highest level of health so Reiki and intuitive wisdom has an unobstructed vessel to flow into and through.

The breath is precious. It is the first thing we do at birth and the last thing we do as we leave the body. During our precious time between birth and death, our breath is the bridge between the physical and the non-physical. Right at this moment, really feel your own breath in a new way.

Feel the truth of your breath being a precious bridge, a living, pumping mechanism. Every single breath that we take is drawing the energy of the Universe into the physical body. Its mechanism is so important that the breath is the only body system that we can alter immediately. We cannot tell our gall bladder to work faster or our spleen to clean out the toxins more rapidly. We can deliberately hold our breath or make ourselves pant rapidly. We can alter our breath immediately with our thoughts.

Why do we have that choice? Because it is a key to our well-being and a key in our spiritual life. You are a physical body and a spirit at the same time. Your breath is the bridge between the physical being and the non-physical world of the cosmos. This bridge can either be weak or it can be dynamic and vibrant. Conscious breathing is a vital link in the empowerment and use of energy in general. It is also crucial as we become a clear, unencumbered vessel for the force of Reiki and the wisdom of intuition.

YOUR MOMENT OF Self-Awareness Examine this important link in your own body. How do you tend to breathe in your everyday life? How do you use your breath during Reiki sessions for others? Do you consciously direct your breath during Reiki sessions? Write down the instant details of your awareness.

Human Toroidal Field

Along with our breath and breathing patterns, let's look at a particularly effective energy pattern for every single living human being. This energy pattern, called the human toroidal field, is directed by our breath and it is like taking our daily shower. This information is not just for energy workers or Reiki practitioners. This information will assist all of us as vital, healthy, spiritual, and physical beings.

Science has recognized that the human energy field moves in a formation that is called the toroidal field. When I came across images of the toroidal field on the Internet, I almost jumped out of my chair with surprise. I saw a diagram showing a fountain of energy flowing upward through a human form. The diagram is exactly the way I perceive energy flowing though people who are exceptionally well physically, mentally, and emotionally. I could not believe that a few scientists think that human energy moves in the same way that I have intuitively witnessed for years! I love when science and the non-physical blend together.

On the next page is a simplified diagram of the healthiest movement of the human energy field. One man in my workshop saw the diagram as a type of enclosure around the body. Do not see this diagram as a cage around the body. The diagram is not meant to show an encapsulating form around each human. This image is meant to display the upward directional flow, exactly like that of a fountain. The upward flow creates a form much like a fountain out in a pond of water. The pump for the human fountain is your breath. As the human energy field rises upward with each breath, it fills the body and expands out beyond the lines on this drawing to shine bright and large without any limits.

Note: A different teacher might have asked you to direct your energy downward. If this is the case, I ask you to at least try the toroidal field as I explain on the following pages and notice any differences you might experience.

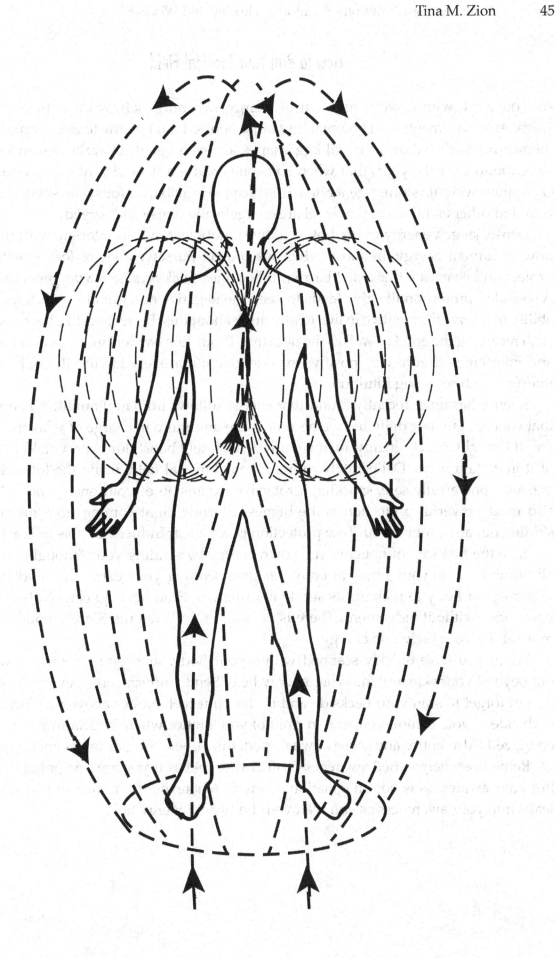

How to Run Your Toroidal Field

As you work with it, your fountain of energy will purposely work with you in many ways. As I have mentioned before in my other books, I am not one to ask people to protect themselves with bubbles, crystal egg shapes, or even beautiful walls. As an intuitive, I have found over the years that when someone creates a wall of protection, even if it is a crystalline wall, it is often generated from fear, suspicion, jealousy, or similar emotions. Fear and other emotions at that level are energetically dense and jagged.

Dense, jagged energy created by negative emotions tends to interfere with the natural flow of human energy. In short, when we protect ourselves out of fear, eventually the protection becomes a thickened barrier. It becomes thick *because* it was generated in fear. A so-called protection like this tends to keep the negative out, but also interferes with our ability to receive the positive in life. Really think about this. Protection-like barriers interfere with receiving the good as well as the negative. Protective barriers grow thicker and thicker and interfere with receiving positive experiences in our everyday life. These barriers also interfere with receiving intuition.

Science has more recently found that energy follows human thought. When we apply that concept into our daily life we become more and more in charge of who and what we are. If thought directs energy, then we can deliberately boost our energy field by thinking of it in certain ways. Deliberately running your toroidal field, using the following steps, creates a powerfully safe, sparkling protective expansion of your energy field. Your true and most powerful protection is the bigness of your Light coming from inside of you, shining out and around you. True protection is not a fear induced bubble or barrier.

Take the first step of noticing your own energy by sending your "thought awareness" all around inside your physical body. Imagine sending your ears, eyes, and finger tips around your body to pick up its subtle information. Scan very quickly. Notice whatever you notice without judgement. There is no way to do it wrong. Simply notice and learn more about your body and energy.

When you have quickly scanned within your body, send your "thought awareness" out beyond your skin, out into your energy field. Send your sensors in every direction and do not forget to scan your backside and under your feet. Notice above you, beneath you, each side of you, behind you, and in front of you. Notice where it feels strong, bright, and energized. Also notice any sense of weakened, thin, open, torn, or lower energetic areas.

Remember: heightened awareness will always feel as if you are imagining everything, but your awareness is not imagination. Go with whatever you notice and trust whatever leaps into your awareness as you scan your body and energy field.

YOUR MOMENT OF

Self-Awareness

Accept and trust whatever springs into your thoughts as you run your eyes, ears, and fingertip sensors past your skin and all around your field. Write down the instant details of your awareness.

_____

_____

_____

_____

_____

_____

_____

_____

_____

_____

_____

You might find that most of your field is rich with energy, but weak in certain places. You might become aware that your energy field has openings, tears, or thin areas, and you might also have rich full bright areas. Any type of weakened condition indicates the need for immediate action to bolster the natural protection that your field provides for you.

Look at the drawing of the toroidal as you read the following description. Imagine your energy field responding and flowing in this manner. Feel that you are in charge of you, your body, and your energy. Deliberately take charge of your energy by thinking and knowing that energy follows your thoughts. Now that you have assessed your body and energy field, and know where the weak areas are, you can cleanse and protect your physical being and your energetic essence.

Begin by simply breathing in your normal pattern, but this time notice all the sensations of your breath. Feel the breath entering into your nose, throat, and chest. Notice all the physical sensations. Shift your awareness to your feet. Imagine inhaling through the soles of your feet. Let the energy build playfully and joyfully. Focus your thoughts to see and feel rainbows rising up through your feet with each inhalation. The full spectrum of the visible colors of the rainbow are pure and cleansing.

Now allow gold to intermingle with your rainbows. Consider the precious element of gold as glimmers and twinkles. It is not just a precious element from the earth. Gold also has its own precious energetic frequency. It vibrates at a distinctly elevated frequency, which is innately protective. The dark or negative cannot come near bright golden light because of its elevated pulsing vibration. Allow the golden frequency to sizzle—yes, sizzle—with golden sparks throughout your field. Allow the gold to mingle and interlace with your rainbows each time you inhale.

Deliberately send rainbows and golden sparkles up your legs equally, filling you as they rise higher into the trunk of your body. That expansion builds and flows like a fountain, filling your organs, muscles, bones, spine, heart, and head. You are so full of rainbows that you shine through every inch of your skin. Do not forget the backside of your body. The back of you from toes to crown must shine and shimmer equally. The human back is often the area most vulnerable to the influence of negativity.

Now deliberately send rainbows and gold into your energy field. With your thoughts, send both into any weakened areas that you found during your initial self-scan. When you are very full of this strength and vigor inside and outside and around you, allow that fullness to rise up and out the crown of your head. Watch it shoot up into your higher self and then into the heavens. Then, like a fountain, your energy and energy of the heavens, together, flows back down into your body and your energy field and back into the earth.

This natural flow continues to cycle in a constant motion up through your body and spine every time you inhale. Your breath is like a pump in a fountain. Pump yourself up with rainbows until you are so full that they rise out of the crown of your head in very gentle ways. Send your energy up into the universe, higher and higher. You are tapping into the energetic matrix of the universe. Allow the universe to shower its finest empowerment and intelligence back into your energy field and your aura. Allow your body to feel the sensations of this flow. Ever so gently feel this beauty and power rain down into your mind, body, and energy field, and enter again into the earth. As you think it, your body will simply feel the sensations of being part of the universal collective of energy, the aliveness and the intelligence that has collected over the centuries.

You are electrifying not only your body but also your eternal being. Think, picture, and feel that your entire force field is cleansed, invincible, and electrified with rainbows and gold. The energy will give you warm vitality and the sense of taking a perfect heavenly shower.

The goal is to practice until you can generate the full cycle of your fountain in just a few seconds and without any effort. The purpose of the rainbow vibration is to break up and disintegrate thickened, dense energy in order to cleanse and heal the body and the field. The purpose of the electrified golden energy is to power up your natural force field so that anything negative will simply bounce off and away.

People will become aware of your calm confidence and your empowerment. Deliberately running your toroidal field in this precise manner will replenish your auric field and create the most intense protection for you without creating a single wall or barrier between you and the world around you. Practice and practice some more to achieve a perfect pulsating shower of earth and heaven, truly connected and safe.

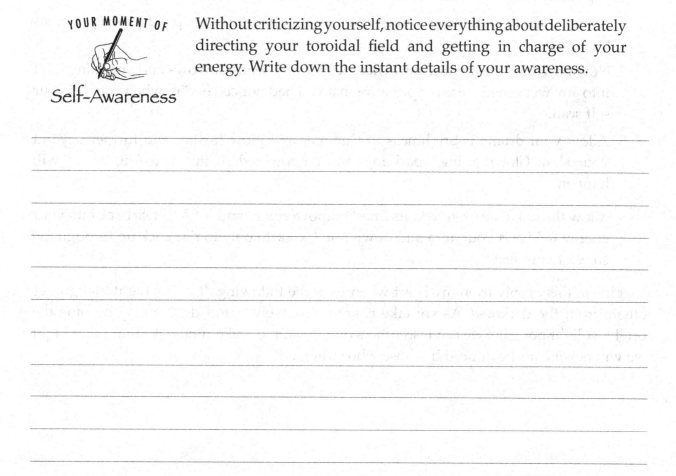

YOUR MOMENT OF

Self-Awareness

Without criticizing yourself, notice everything about deliberately directing your toroidal field and getting in charge of your energy. Write down the instant details of your awareness.

Nine Steps to Build Your Toroidal Field

Here are the most basic steps to run your energy in the toroidal field formation. It will release your old thickened barriers, sparkle and shine up your energy, and enlarge your field to create the most potent protection of all—your human toroidal field. You are not meant to be a weakened link in the system. You are meant to be a powerful bridge between heaven and earth.

1. Do not make this hard or time consuming. Think it and the energy will naturally follow your thoughts instantly.

2. Scan your body and energy field looking for weakened areas but also noticing your strong areas. Remember to scan the entire length of your backside from head to heel too.

3. Imagine inhaling through the soles of your feet as well as your heart.

4. Imagine inhaling rainbows and sizzling gold into the soles of your feet.

5. Become so full of rainbows and gold that they shine through every inch of your skin. Especially remember to shine through your entire backside.

6. Focus on sending rainbows and gold into all low energy areas, painful areas, or areas that are ill.

7. Now power up your entire auric field. Especially send rainbows and sparkling gold into any weakened areas in your aura that you had noticed earlier when you did your self scan.

8. Allow your dramatic brightness to shimmer and glow further and further beyond your skin. Glowing, big, sparkling, and empowered. Think it, feel it, and it will happen.

9. Allow the universe to shower its finest empowerment and intelligence back into your energy field and your aura and down into the earth only to rise back up through the soles of your feet.

I mean this deeply from my heart when I say the following: It is our Light that guides others from the darkness. As we take charge of ourselves and deliberately become the brightest light possible, we can lead others on the path to wakefulness. Without that Light we will never even be noticed by those who struggle.

CHAPTER 6

Be the Intuitive You Are Meant to Be

Intuition is the ability to notice non-physical information that we humans are naturally created to receive. In fact, we are naturally wired to be intuitive. We cannot stop being intuitive, but we can become excellent at ignoring it! People, in general, have become so good at blocking intuition that they are instantly terrified when an intuitive wisdom does happen to get past all the barriers and pop into their consciousness.

Reiki and intuition are not separate from each other. Reiki is the loving, healing life force of the Universe we dwell in. Intuition is simply information within and from the life force of the Universe. Intuition is the ability to understand something immediately without the need for conscious reasoning. The Cambridge Dictionary states intuition is the ability to understand or know something without needing to think about it or use reason to discover it. It is that simple. We humans walk, run, drive, sit, sleep, breathe, and eat in a colossal, limitless, and organized structure of energy and information. This is the profound nature of the Universe and the profound nature of we humans dwelling in that Universe.

Personal Story: Lori Irvin, Medical Intuitive

Since I was little, I knew I was powerful, I just didn't know how. This mysterious feeling, this knowing, seemed really scary to me as a little girl. So for protection, I did not allow my gifts until one day, I finally followed my intuition and put this powerful gift into practice.

It happened when I was taking a beginning intuition class, and the lesson of the day was to learn how to receive confirmation from Spirit. A fellow student, Sally, arrived and said she was in pain from a recent abdominal surgery but did not want to miss class. Trying to ease her pain, she sat cross-legged on the floor. My intuition told me to go over to her. I was curious and bewildered, responding internally, "What can I do? I don't want to bother her." But the feeling that I needed to help her was so palpable and demanding, it propelled me to move! I got up and went over to her. My intuition guided me to stand behind her and float my hand above her lower back and feel for energy. I didn't even know what I was searching for, but I found a warm sensation emanating from her left side just above her hip bone. As the warmth progressed to heat, I instinctively started "pulling" that energy away from Sally's body. It was like I was in my own world, just a world of Sally, this energy, and me following my intuition.

I lost the awareness of time, and the hum of the class seemed like it was in another dimension (or was I?). Sally said she felt better and did not want me to miss out on the lesson, so she quietly got up and went to another part of the room and laid down on her back. Again, my intuition told me to follow her since she continued to display signs of pain. I sat on a chair next to her and began feeling for energy in her abdominal area. I felt that same kind of heat energy. It was beginning to feel familiar, but this time I had to search harder for it as it was elusive at times.

Finally, I located it, and my intuition or Spirit told me to begin swirling my flat palm above her abdominal area and pulling up. As I pulled up the heat with the palm of my hand, I began to rise from a seated to a standing position, all the while consistently feeling the intense heat. At that moment, another classmate told me she could see the energy I was pulling out. She described it as an off-green, cone-shaped spiral whirling up from Sally's body with the point directed into my hand. As I continued this process and pulled the energy all the way up with me on my tip-toes with my arm at its highest elevation, I intuitively knew to release this pain energy into the ground. This release of the energy, which I have discovered in my continued studies, is the act of discarding that energy into Mother Earth for her to transmute into love.

When I asked Sally what she experienced, she said, "It is a difficult feeling to explain, but it suddenly felt as if the pain was being pulled right out of my body. I could feel it moving out and away from me toward the sky. And the pain was gone! Then I opened my eyes to see you standing directly above me, rising onto your tiptoes and slowly raising your hand over your head, using the same pulling motion that I had intuitively been feeling with my body." At that moment, we both knew without speaking what had happened, and I began to cry. Obviously, this was an incredibly profound experience for both of us.

I continue to take classes to learn and grow. When I took the Holy-Fire Reiki Master Teacher Classes, I just kept saying, "I already do this, I already know this. How can this be?" My Reiki teacher told me I already knew this process because I was given the ability to use it before I learned it in this lifetime. Spirit works in miraculous ways!

Since then, I have been using several techniques including Reiki and this innate pulling-extraction technique to help people heal physically, emotionally, and spiritually. It is such a beautiful gift and I continue to deepen and develop this gift so I may better serve others.

When focusing on growth and development, I find it is incredibly important to learn how to be the best conduit for Spirit, as this allows our special gifts to come through. On that note, one of the most instrumental classes in my development journey was Tina Zion's medical intuition class. It proved to be a real turning point for me as it propelled me to start my own healing practice. (Tina, my clients and I thank you!)

So, to *all* of you reading this book, please continue to follow your intuition. Do not be afraid. Jump off that cliff and you will find that you can fly! As you try it, intend it, and practice it, your innate gifts will come to the surface and you will truly be on your life's path. It's time to fly!

Lori Irvin, Medical Intuitive
ZSourceConnection.com
Lorredd@hotmail.com

Becoming intuitive is simply the deliberate, conscious decision to notice. It is not magical or mystical. Intuition is the most natural mechanism of perceiving, and you are wired to do it. You are an antenna for intuitive information. Antennae do not put forth any effort at all. They just sit there and receive effortlessly. As a human you have a choice to receive it or block it out and be terrified of it.

Everyone wonders how to distinguish between thoughts from their thinking mind and intuition. How can we tell them apart? We are thinking beings, but intuition senses non-physical knowledge that does not come from our logical thinking brain. When we have an issue to figure out or a decision to make, our thinking mind moves in every direction, trying to find the best answer. Your thinking mind might say at the exact same time, "Yes, I can do that, but no, maybe I better not." Can you see how your thinking mind just told you two different things at the same time and even in the same sentence?

Intuition is steady, calm, whispery, and will consistently give the same information over and over again about a single topic or issue. Now notice the difference. "Every time I try to decide about this issue my brain goes all over the place, but I continually keep sensing or feeling that I should do it." Notice how the intuitive awareness does not fluctuate about a topic.

Six Keys for Your Intuitive Success

Key 1 Intuition will always feel like imagination because it is usually non-physical and processed through the right side of the brain which is the creative side. Intuition will always feel like you are making it up. Make the leap right now by understanding that intuitive information will constantly and always feel like make believe. It will always seem like you are inventing it or simply dreaming it up.

Key 2 Absolutely trust what you receive no matter what, even if you do not understand it. Simply describe what you intuitively notice. It is very important that you describe what you received in exact detail to the client.

Key 3 Do not interpret what you receive. It is the interpretation of information that gets us into trouble. If you are receiving intuitive information about yourself, then by all means interpret it. But if you are working with another person, refrain from interpreting or trying to explain the insights that you are receiving. When you try to interpret intuitive information for another, you are actually interjecting your own personal experience into theirs. Interpretations come from your thinking mind as it tries to make sense of an image, a word, a phrase, or a symbol for another person. Allow the receiver to tell you what it means to them. They will surprise you and tell you that they know exactly what it means and how it relates to their struggles.

Key 4   And now for the grandest and most hidden key of all . . . our expectations! If we expect something to happen in a certain way and if that something happens in a different way, we will miss the event completely. We will miss the intuitive information because we were focused on something else. We missed the true intuitive information because we were waiting on the way we thought it should be. An expectation is a strong thought that restricts all other possibilities.

Intuitive information bombards us every minute of the day and night. If you think intuition must look a certain way or behave in a certain manner, vast dimensions of vital information are escaping you. If intuition does not come in the form or path you expect, then you will completely miss all the other pathways it is coming to you. This is a crucial point for success as an intuitive Reiki practitioner! The most important thing I can say here is to expect the most unexpected.

Key 5   Intuitive information also shows itself to us in physical form. Intuition consists of non-physical wave lengths of data that comes to us from all directions. For example, I was once sitting in my car at a busy intersection contemplating an issue in my life. I closed my eyes for a few seconds and asked Spirit for direct guidance that I would not be able to miss. Just as I opened my eyes, a large truck flew through the intersection with one word painted in giant letters across the truck. It was exactly what I was hoping for and it was the answer to my dilemma!

Key 6   Everything in the world around us has meaning. Intuitive information is absolutely everywhere. We simply must allow ourselves to notice. People will use the term synchronicity when two unrelated events happen that make a great deal of sense to us but at the same time we know that they should not have coincided as they did. A coincidence is another term used to describe unexpected occurrences happening. Notice those moments now as meaningful, and notice the wonderment and wisdom of the world you live in. Incorporate intuition into your daily life and be playful with it.

Remember: We cannot stop being intuitive, but we can become excellent at ignoring it!

YOUR MOMENT OF

Self-Awareness

Notice the message in each of the primary keys. What stands out to you in each key? Write down the instant details of your awareness.

Key 1

_____

_____

Key 2

_____

_____

Key 3

_____

_____

Key 4

_____

_____

Key 5

_____

_____

_____

Key 6

_____

_____

_____

Tips to Explain Intuition and Reiki to Others

It is fearful people and yes, even some Reiki master-teachers, who make Reiki and intuition an enigma. It is fearful people who decide that intuition has no place in a Reiki session. It is fearful people who have decided that Reiki and intuition create a complex, mysterious, problematic situation in the healing room. The two, in fact, cannot be separated. Intuition and Reiki are a union of healing and wisdom given to us from the cosmos.

When fear of Reiki and fear of intuition rises up from those around you, it is time for you to step into the calm and patient teacher role and completely trust yourself. Be matter of fact and do not show any emotion. Hold that demeanor and describe Reiki and intuition both as electricity charging up a battery in a flashlight or in an automobile. Humans are like a battery and with use, they lose some of their charge. Reiki and intuition are battery chargers for people!

Share the following: The medical field has developed multiple tests that measure the electricity in the human body. EEGs, EKGs, and EMGs are all measuring electrical movement in the brain, heart, and muscles. Explain that the nervous system are the electrical cords that allow electricity to flow from brain to body and back to the brain. Explain that on television they have seen emergency responders putting paddles on a person's chest and yell, "Stand back!" Electricity is used to start a person's heart. They use electricity because an electrical spark sets off every beat of our heart during normal life. So it makes sense that a jolt of electricity from the machine will stimulate the beat to begin again.

Confidently summarize that Reiki is like a battery charger for people, and you have learned how to help people get their batteries charged! By clearly and confidently answering questions those around you have about Reiki, you will help them feel more at ease with energy work.

YOUR MOMENT OF

Self-Awareness

What have you become aware of as you read this last section? Practice explaining what Reiki is to two or three people and watch their fear subside as you explain it as electricity. Write down the instant details of your awareness.

_____

_____

_____

_____

_____

_____

Always Ask for Permission

When I lived on the Navajo reservation in New Mexico I participated in many Native American sweat lodges. One night after an intense sweat with ten other people, the medicine man walked up to me and gave me a long hug. This was the first time he had given me a hug. I immediately felt his energy penetrate me sexually. Please realize that he did not do this physically but energetically. I had participated in twelve or more sweats with this man and I was shocked that he would abuse his energetic abilities. Sexually violating me on the energetic level is just as real as a violation on a physical level. It is real and it is disrespectful, intrusive, and abusive. He was taking advantage of me and probably other participants who came to him in trust that night. I was not asked permission and I would not have given it.

Many years later my Facebook Reiki page blew up with emotional comments when I said that Reiki practitioners must ask their clients for permission before a session and they must also ask permission before giving distant Reiki. I had no idea that asking Reiki people to ask their clients for permission before a Reiki session would generate such turmoil. I was shocked! Basically, people posted that they never need to ask permission of anyone because Reiki can never do harm. I agreed that was a good point, but due to all the emotional reactions my primary point was overlooked.

You too might be asking, "Well, why is it necessary to ask permission if Reiki can never do any harm?" My answer is this. If we send Reiki or even a traditional prayer to someone, it will not be received as deeply as possible and may even bounce off the person who is not readily open to it. The active participation of the receiver is important, even on an energetic level. When the person accepts, whether verbally or energetically, a larger, wider, more flowing channel opens. The possibility of a more powerful exchange of energy escalates. Permission greatly enhances the delivery of Reiki because the energy channel is unrestricted by other emotions.

There is another reason to ask permission: respect. Sincere respect for the individual—their feelings, personal space, and wishes—is of paramount importance. I am strongly committed to be honorable and ethically strong while working with Reiki and with energy in general. These values will hold you in the Light for your clients.

There are multiple ways to ask for permission prior to a healing. I recommend you use at least one of the three mentioned below:

1. Simply ask them directly, either face-to-face or over the phone.

2. If the person is lying on your table, be sure to ask permission to begin. This gives the person a feeling of really participating in what is about to happen.

3. Ask the client intuitively. Sit for just a second, the same way you do in prayer or meditation, and in your mind ask that person for permission. Then wait another second to listen and feel. You will get a "feeling" of a no or yes. The feeling might be an image in your mind's eye of that person giving you some kind of a signal. For example, you may see the person smile at you in your mind's eye. The smile is signaling yes, of course. A yes response might be a wave of hello to you. The person may shake their head no. An image of the person walking away from you suggests a refusal. Do not kid yourself into thinking that it is okay to proceed no matter what signal you receive. Function with the highest integrity possible. A client's trust should *never* be violated.

Personal Story: Anne Ruthmann

I learned through distance healing work that people must be willing and open to receiving, and that it is possible for people to block themselves from receiving healing energy. This is why distance healing work, or any energy healing work, requires permission and an open exchange between client and practitioner. You can't go around just trying to heal a bunch of people or read their energy at a distance when they don't want it and aren't actively putting themselves in a place of receiving. You can do things like praying and sending a little extra helpful energy that kind of hangs out in the ether waiting to be accepted when they ask for it and are open to receiving it, but you can't assume any healing will be received unless a client has invited that healing energy for themselves first and foremost. Because Reiki energy will never enter someone's unwelcoming energy field, Reiki and distance healing can only be helpful and beneficial when welcomed. You cannot force Reiki healing energy on anyone; it can only be invited.

Anne Ruthmann
www.anneruthmann.com
anneruthmann@gmail.com

YOUR MOMENT OF

Self-Awareness

Write down thoughts that you are having as you read my thoughts regarding permission. Please practice intuitively asking for permission to send Reiki to two or three people at a distance right now. Be especially aware of the different ways people respond to your intuitive question and how you perceive a yes or a no from them. Write down the instant details of your awareness.

_____

_____

_____

_____

_____

_____

_____

_____

_____

_____

_____

_____

CHAPTER 7
Take Action as an Intuitive

Intuitive Expectations

This is probably the most important section of all. Please examine your own thoughts and experiences as you continue to read this portion. We human beings receive intuition constantly, yet most people are adamant that they never have an intuitive moment in their lives. How can that possibly be? It is because most people do not identify the intuitive information they receive as such. Most people think it is just their brain or wild imagination firing off weird ideas or strange images. Others simply reject the moment and avoid ever thinking of the intuitive experience ever again.

Remember: We are all naturally intuitive, but most people excel at discounting intuitive experiences as nothing.

I want to help you know and understand what intuitive experiences you might be experiencing already and what your intuition can give to you if you allow yourself to notice it. We discussed what intuition really is and six key concepts for your intuitive success in Chapter 6. So where to begin?

Begin by remembering all the experiences you have been trying to forget. I mean that sincerely. Especially remember any experiences you had while giving Reiki to another person or to an animal. Remember any subtle or not so subtle impression, sensation, thoughts, or emotions that came up during the Reiki session. I do not care what the experience is. Just recall it, no matter what you thought it was at the time.

I will give you some examples, but they represent only the most miniscule sample in the never-ending spectrum of possibilities. It is up to you to allow your mind to open all the doorways to the living cosmos, which has no end. Notice all kinds of things that either quickly pop or flow in and out of your awareness.

Most intuitive information will flash by, or you may also receive so many flashes that it seems nearly impossible to keep track of it all. You may see some things with your eyes open or your eyes closed. You may see impressions deep within your mind's eye. As you notice images, also notice a song that suddenly plays in your head and the lyrics repeat over and over; a memory, a symbol, or a knowing may spring up. Notice if suddenly your entire mood changes during the Reiki session. For example, you may feel that life is fun and alive before you give a Reiki session, but during the session a wave of depression rushes into you. You may suddenly inhale more easily as you sense the room filling with angels, or you may feel a presence telling you they are an aunt or uncle of your Reiki client. Feel with your body, hear with your inner ears, realize all things coming to you from the non-physical realms of life. Know inside of your soul that you are a vital part of an entire healing team.

My first intuitive piece of information during a Reiki session came as I placed my hands on a woman's shoulders and instantly saw inside of her lungs. The image in my mind looked exactly like an X-ray of a lung. I could see the inflamed areas of her lungs in my mind's eye and images of her smoking cigarettes. A few weeks later I felt as if I was flying inside of my Reiki client's intestines and finding a group of cancerous polyps. I could hear people arguing and screaming behind another client. Another person radiated the colors of a rainbow, while another had thick colors of a swamp in olive green, brown, and mustard yellow hanging on her back.

Receiving accurate intuitive information only escalated from there. I began picking up bits and pieces of each person's life story. The intuitive information deepened in importance both emotionally and physically. As Reiki poured through me and into each client on my table, I perceived pockets of darkness burst open and break into tiny particles as the fine, pure healing of Reiki energy surged into certain areas. I then watched and felt the area soften in gentle ways then brim with sparkles where the dark was only seconds ago. I heard words as if someone was standing next to me giving me messages to tell my client. Unexplained scenes unfolded like tiny movies, and each scene told an important unknown aspect about my client's struggles.

I was accurately finding physical and emotional conditions such as low levels of vitamin D, broken bones, kidney infections, inflamed bladders, deep depression, suppressed anger, cancer, bulging discs in spines, autoimmune disease, and broken hearts. It never stopped. The vital information kept pouring into my conscious awareness.

I didn't tell any of my Reiki clients. Would it scare them off? Would they believe me? What if it didn't make any sense to them? What if I was wrong? Finally, at the end of her session, I decided to ask one open-minded woman if she would like to hear the intuitive information that I received during her session. Her eyes opened wide and she said, "I would love that. Please tell me everything!" So I told her everything. And I told everything to the next person and the next one and I never hesitated or stopped sharing with anyone again.

As time went on, I also began sharing in greater and greater detail what I noticed. The more detail I described, the more my clients told me how accurate I was. Notice that completely describing the tiniest details of your intuitive awareness is *not* giving a diagnostic label to the client. Unless you are a physician or of another discipline licensed to do so, you cannot give a client a diagnosis. Do not diagnose your clients. Regardless of licensing, however, we can describe in detail what we perceive without stating out loud to the client the actual medical diagnosis. The more detail I described the more my clients told me how accurate I was for them. This is a very important key. Notice that completely describing the tiniest details of your intuitive awareness is extremely different from giving a diagnostic label to the client.

I cannot tell you exactly what will happen for you as an intuitive Reiki healer, but I can tell you that the intuitive information that comes through you will bring many levels of healing for your clients. Do not be afraid to share it with them. People are yearning to understand more about their illnesses and their struggles. People are yearning for help beyond the traditional help that Western medicine can give. Intuitive Reiki does not replace the medical world; it works in conjunction with Western medicine to create truly integrative healthcare.

YOUR MOMENT OF

Self-Awareness

Remember the intuitive information now that you have previously discredited. What techniques have you used to ignore or discredit your abilities? Now truthfully notice the intuitive information that is already coming to you during Reiki sessions. Write down the instant details of your awareness.

Six Pathways to Receive Intuition

The next step is to expect the unexpected and to realize you are a natural antenna for intuitive information. There are many pathways by which information comes to you. All you need to do is to notice all your natural intuitive pathways. Review them while keeping yourself in mind at the same time.

Feelings/Body sensations (Clairsentience). You must know your own physical body prior to offering a Reiki session. Do a quick body scan of yourself so you are aware of your own aches and pains, mood, etc. Notice sensations within your body that instantly change as soon as you begin a Reiki session. Any changes in your own state of being is an energetic signal from your client. You are *not* catching someone's illness. You are getting information *about* someone's illness. When you feel discomfort in your own body, command, "Thank you for the information about my client. It is not mine. Out of me now." Imagine yourself pushing out the discomfort as you state the command. People who consider themselves an empath are clairsentient. Remember to not absorb everyone's pain and suffering. Be the Light and hold the Light for others.

Taste (Clairgustance)/Smell (Clairolfaction). Most energy practitioners pay no attention to these potential channels of information. If the taste or texture in your mouth suddenly changes during the session, it is information about the client and not you. Uncontrolled diabetes might signal you as a sweet, sticky texture in your mouth. You may think you smell something like hot metal, which is a common energy signal of chemotherapy. A heavy musky odor may be telling you that the client is toxic in some way or signal a general illness. Many Reiki healers suddenly smell cigarette smoke even after the client stopped smoking years ago.

Hearing (Clairaudience). You might instantly notice a fleeting sound such as a whisper, the ringing of bells, arguing, or singing. Many times you will receive a voice from Spirit that gives a message to you to give to your Reiki client. You might also hear different tones coming from different areas of the client's chakras or sections of their body.

Knowing (Claircognizance). The best and maybe only way to describe a knowing is when a strong wave rushes through your entire body that gives you a piece of information. One example could be knowing, without seeing it, that a person's solar plexus is dark and empty. Another example might be a rush of feeling abused and victimized but not perceiving the details.

Seeing (Clairvoyance). Most people think that seeing the non-physical realm is the most important pathway. This pathway is no more important than the others. If you think it is the only way to be intuitive, then that only means you are missing all the other pathways that intuition is coming to you. You might see visually or see with your eyes closed inside of your mind's eye. Be aware that seeing can come as flashes of images or appear like a still photo. Visual information can also unfold like a movie showing an entire event.

Many times intuitive information comes to us in a symbol or, in other words, an image that tells a story. Our spirit guides utilize symbols because they are a very efficient way to give us a lot of intuitive information instantly. A few examples might be seeing a country's flag, a broken ladder, a city's skyline in a storm, or a bucket lying on the ground. Make sure you share whatever symbol you see with your client without trying to understand or interpret it. Allow the client to tell you what it might mean to them. You are instantly picking up a piece of that person's life story.

Thoughts (Telepathy). In my experience, this is the most overlooked pathway. People believe that all of their thoughts are of their own making. People struggle to recognize that thoughts bounding and leaping into their minds are intuitive information. Telepathy is communication from one mind to another mind. When you consider science declaring that energy does indeed follow human thought, telepathy is exactly that. We humans are naturally able to send and receive thoughts. The way to tell the difference between your logical thinking mind and receiving telepathic information is this: Your logical thinking mind will ponder or question, and bounce all around trying to make sense of something. Telepathic intuitive thoughts will literally pop, dive, jump, or leap into your mind as if out of nowhere.

YOUR MOMENT OF

Self-Awareness

Review the six pathways one at a time. Evaluate each pathway and notice if it is partially open, completely closed, or wide open and flowing. If any are closed or partially closed, open each one with your commanding thoughts. Be in charge of you and open all your paths. Think it and the energy will follow. Write down the instant details of your awareness.

Feelings/Body sensations

_____

_____

_____

Taste/Smell

_____

_____

Hearing

_____

_____

Knowing

_____

_____

Seeing

_____

_____

Thoughts

_____

_____

Using All the Pathways

I have known many professional intuitives in my life and they all use the term "seeing" in a very loose, general way. I have used "see" in a similar way. "Seeing" has become a shortened slang word for "perceiving." Intuitives and mediums all around the world use "seeing" as a catch-all term. This slang word has created a false idea for people that they must see everything. These same people are convinced they are not intuitive because they do not see everything. I am pretty good at intuitive perception and healing but even I only "see" a portion of what is happening because I am receiving intuitive information through all of my pathways. When intuitives say they "saw" something, they could mean:

- An intuitive thought energy popping into their mind. This is telepathy.

- Body sensations that are not their own, but energetic signatures from others.

- Sounds coming from the client's energy field.

- Unusual smells filling the room.

- Spirit directing their focus and informing them of what to do next.

- The knowing that flows through them.

- And a myriad of other pieces of information.

Seeing is only one pathway. If you keep focusing on seeing everything, that only means you are missing all the other insights that are traveling to you through other routes. All pathways are equally relevant and vitally important.

I am begging you to notice all the pathways of intuitive perception. All of them. When you focus on information coming in through the other routes, your visual abilities will relax and then naturally open because you no longer push to see. Relaxation will remove the constriction of working too hard to accomplish something. Intuition passively and naturally flows through our pathways. You simply need to take notice when the intuitive information arrives. I am not over simplifying when I say that your primary job as an intuitive is to notice and notice some more. Notice the tiniest details from all of your pathways.

Some examples of how I have experienced intuition arriving on various pathways during Reiki sessions include feeling pain in my body but knowing it was a signal of pain in the client's body. I would smell cigarettes even though the person had stopped smoking years ago. I could feel that a portion or organ of a client's body was closed off, darkened, or thick, and then instantly Reiki blasted it open, warmed it up, and released the pain. A client's guardian angel would send him or her a message by telepathically sending it into my mind. After the session ended, I would verbally give the client the message. I have witnessed stunningly beautiful spirit beings lean over and kiss my client's third eye during a session. I have seen cracked, broken hearts in my clients' chests and watched white hands with golden needle and thread sewing the crack back together. Do not discount any pathway that intuitive information might travel to you. The possibilities for intuitive information coming to you are uncountable.

Reiki Spirit Guide Specialists

I had just received my second attunement. I was told that I had a Reiki master guide who would lead my healing sessions, and I saw him standing before me. When I intuitively asked him for his name, he told me to call him Raku. I had never heard the word before. When asked about my guide by the teacher, I informed her that my guide's name was Raku. She looked perplexed and asked if I was sure I received the name correctly.

"Yes," I said. "He was very clear and sent his name into my mind telepathically. I also saw it spelled out in my mind." I went on to describe him in detail as he stood smiling at me. Months later, I was shocked that not only did I receive a name for my guide that was also the name of a Reiki symbol, but I also described him exactly as Mikao Usui appears in his photos. In truth, this was only one of the many enchanting shocks that Reiki brought into my life.

There are many energetic healing modalities to learn and to use. In my experience, Reiki is one of the only modalities that allows, and even asks, practitioners to turn a healing over to Spirit. If you allow it and get out of the way, Reiki, the universal life force, truly is in charge of the healing treatment. We practitioners are not in charge.

Many of the other modalities are based on learning to follow various techniques with numerous steps and rules. Most of the other teachings are based on a doctrine and training the students specific ways of doing certain steps, certain hand positions, and certain actions. The modalities that have many guidelines are absolutely fine and many healers truly appreciate having certain steps to follow.

Reiki does not seem to have any rules. Your intuition (which is information from the non-physical realms) guides you toward what to do, how long to do it, and where to place your hands. Even the hand positions that are widely written about are only suggestions and a basis to begin. In my experience, the more the healer gets out of their own way, the more intense the healing becomes, and the more insightful the intuitive information becomes.

Our role as an intuitive Reiki healer is to be the purest, clearest, unobstructed instrument for the energy to pulse through. We are an important link in the healing system of this universe. Believe it or not, we hold an important position in healing situations as a necessary connection or link between the Universe and the recipient needing the healing. I used to struggle wondering why the Universe, Spirit, angels, or guides do not just heal people when they need it or when they asked for it. For a long, long time I kept questioning why healers were even needed. Why doesn't healing happen if the person in need just asks for it?

The answer to my struggle just popped in one day. I was informed that we healers are a valuable part of the structure of the Universe. We are a required and essential link in the universal system of health and well-being. If we could do everything ourselves, then we would become islands with less of a motivation to connect with others. This was my breakthrough in understanding! Did you get it? *We healers are a required and essential link in the universal system of health and well-being.* Our spirit guides need us as much as we need them to create powerful links in the healing system.

Sometimes it seems that Spirit is waiting patiently for us to become aware of them. Spirit is ready and willing to respond to our requests, but the secret is that we have to ask for it. This is a world of choice and to struggle alone or to ask for divine assistance is one component amid the vast number of daily choices we have. Choice may be a blessing and sometimes it may seem a curse. Choice, when handled with awareness, is a gift in life. The more we choose with awareness, the smoother life becomes. That awareness comes to us in the form of instinct, intuition, and experience. So, whether to ask for assistance during your Reiki healings or to work alone is up to you.

Not only are they patient, but spirit guides also come in many forms and are diversified in talent and focus. Some of your guides will be with you forever; others come and go depending on your needs and interests. Even if you are already aware of your current guides, please realize that you might also have a Reiki spirit guide specialist you can call on. You might also have a specialist for intuitive wisdom. You might have a guide for accurate intuition, and you could have a different guide for Reiki healing, or your guide could be excellent at Reiki and also intuition. You might even have a team of specialists with one spokesperson or everyone takes turns informing and assisting you. My hope is that you become aware that there are multitudes of options in the non-physical realm. Just as we have specialists in most professions here on earth, these spirit specialists have dedicated their soul essence in specific areas.

Because this is a world of choice, we must call out to the Universe for a specific type of assistance. When we call out we must be very careful and use our words wisely. By that I mean do not just call out for help. Remember, if energy follows our thoughts then we must choose our words wisely and precisely. We must create an extremely specifically worded request for what we want or need. When we create that specifically worded request, an exact energy pulsates out into the Universe. If we are not selective and specific, then we will not get a selective and specific reply. If we call out in vague, formless words, the Universe will respond with vagueness.

Inviting spirit guides is an excellent example of the mechanics of the Universe. For instance, if we simply call out saying, "I need help!" we could get a spirit guide who thinks they might be able to help. But are they a Reiki or intuitive or diagnostic specialist who excels at working with humans to heal? They won't be if you do not specify that. Again, if we ask for a guide in general vague terms, we will get something general and vague in response.

When we think and call out using explicit descriptive words, we will receive a specific guide. You can be assured that you are inviting in a positive assistant who represents the Light of Source. Examples of a few power words are pure, holy, sacred, compassionate, loving, healer, blessed, radiant, kind, from Source, full of light, and love.

Invite a guide who excels at the highest level of medical understanding, healing, medical diagnosis, energy work, intuitive vision, or all of the above. For instance, asking for the most sacred and pure Reiki specialist who excels in healing humans (or animals) at all levels will give you a remarkable healing teammate.

YOUR MOMENT OF

Self-Awareness

What type of intuitive Reiki guide specialist do you want to work with? What particular power words express what you want? Choose your descriptive words with care. Write down the instant details of your awareness.

Eight Steps to Call Your Reiki Guide Specialist

1. Predetermine and write down what you want in your guide. Use the power words to make sure the Universe responds with the most positive and brightest assistance of all. Remember, energy follows every single thought you have and it follows every single command that you send out.

2. State your command out loud or within your mind. Repeat the command if that feels right to you and feel it deeply within you.

3. Remember that intuition will *always* feel like it is your imagination, but it is real.

4. Notice that your attention will be drawn in a certain direction. Wait and notice everything as it unfolds.

5. Allow the guide to come to you and allow them to come in any form. Do not disregard the guide if it is different than you expected. Always allow the unexpected.

6. Begin to communicate telepathically. Allow your thoughts and their thoughts to transfer back and forth between you. Ask for a name and accept whatever leaps into your mind. Ask questions and accept the thoughts that rush into you mind.

7. Develop an ongoing relationship with your guides. Do not wait until you are in a Reiki session with someone and then try to work with your specialists. Do not wait. Interact together every day so you will be able to work together as a team long before you walk into your sacred Reiki room.

8. Do not doubt or discredit anything about the experience you had when you call out for your specialists. The more you trust them, the more they will excel for you. The more you give thanks to them, the more they involve themselves with you.

YOUR MOMENT OF Self-Awareness

Do not work hard at trying to make this connection. It is all about passively noticing and not working hard at anything. Use your precise powerful words and call out to the Universe. Then notice, notice, and notice some more. Communicate telepathically back and forth with each other. Write down the instant details of your awareness.

_____

_____

_____

_____

Keys for Intuitive Accuracy

Now that you're aware of the many pathways through which intuitive information can be offered to you, and you have spirit guides to assist you, you're well equipped to receive accurate intuitive information. Here are six keys that summarize how to receive intuitive information accurately.

1. The intuitive wisdom that comes to you will always and forever feel like you just imagined or dreamed it up. Know right now that it is real but will constantly feel like a daydream.

2. Do not work hard to notice. There is no work involved at all. You are a passive antenna built and made to be an intuitive receiver.

3. Get out of the way and allow your intuitive Reiki specialty guides to do the work they are meant to do. You are part of a team working together.

4. Do not try to interpret what you receive. Notice every single detail of all the intuitive information that comes to you. Share those details with your client, but do not interpret what you receive. Inform your client and ask what the details mean to them. Their interpretation is more important because your interpretation will be influenced by your personal life. Their own interpretation will be spot on about their life.

5. Your emotions will get in the way of Reiki and will dramatically inhibit your intuitive abilities. Do not offer to do intuitive work for family members or anyone else you have emotions or strong concerns about. You know too much and are too invested in the outcome. You will not be able to get past what you hope will happen. It's impossible to be a neutral and clear passive vessel for intuitive Reiki when deep emotions are involved. The most pristine, accurate intuitive wisdom comes through us when we hold the most neutral passive energetic frequency.

6. To prepare yourself to notice all your pathways of intuition, ask yourself the following questions at the beginning of every Reiki session:

   - How do I suddenly feel emotionally?

   - What changes do I instantly feel in my own body? (These are only energy signatures of your client and not your own issues.)

   - What do I suddenly know that seems to come out of nowhere?

   - What do I notice the Reiki energy truly doing?

   - Are there distant sounds around the person?

   - What colors appear or what colors leap into my mind in word form?

   - Where are the colors located in and around the client's body? Are they dull or bright?

   - Are there any places on this person that seem low or high in energy?

   - What energy movement or lack of movement is there, and where?

   - What am I noticing about the person's general vitality?

   - Do I suddenly smell something that was not there before?

   - Is there any sense of other people involved with this person's life either negatively or positively?

   - Are there any other human spirits or celestial entities present in the room?

I hope you get a sense from these comprehensive questions about how they might lead you to a broader level of awareness.

Specific Steps to Receive Intuitive Wisdom

1. Do not try hard to do anything. Only passively notice whatever you notice.

2. There is no way to do this wrong—simply notice.

3. Your eyes can be open or closed, whatever is comfortable for you.

4. Remember that intuition is non-physical, so it will always feel like your imagination.

5. Sit, notice your thoughts, and then quiet your mind.

6. Feel yourself more as a soul energy and less of a physical body.

7. Stop all thoughts of self. Direct all awareness to the person you are assisting.

8. Using the power words, invite your spirit guide specialist to assist you specifically for your intuitive Reiki session.

9. Ask your Reiki guide to create a safe, secure, sacred space completely around you and the person you are working with.

10. Ask for permission (verbally or intuitively) to begin the session (in person or distant). Wait for a response. Inform the person that you will not be talking unless they speak and you will respond. Inform your client that quiet will help them receive the most benefit from Reiki.

11. Using your breath like a pumping mechanism, inhale Reiki and fill yourself completely with the life force before beginning each session. You only offer Reiki to your clients. Never give your own energy to them.

12. When you are completely bursting with the universal life force of Reiki, allow it to flow through you and into the receiving person.

    Face-to-face session: Envelope the client with Reiki and then allow it to go deep into the physical body.

    Phone or distant session: Send Reiki outward toward their name and their voice. Repeat their name over and over in your mind as you project outward.

13. Allow Reiki to lead the session and to completely direct placement of your hands.

14. At the same time, you will notice and remember the intuitive information that comes to you. Notice all of your pathways of reception. Notice instant sensations/physical feelings within your own body. It is information about them, not you. Notice any instant thoughts, images or colors, knowings, waves of certain emotions, smells, or sounds.

15. Do not make intuition the goal for the Reiki session. Allow Reiki to have its goal as you also passively receive intuitive information.

16. When you feel the surge of Reiki subside with each hand position, move to another position. When you sense Reiki subsiding in general, then bring the session to a close. Inform your client that the session has ended and give them time to rise from the table.

17. Ask the person if they would like to know what you experienced during the session. (You do not need to call it intuition). People will be excited because deep down they know this is real. They are also yearning for different ways to receive help. Inform them what you experienced as Reiki progressed throughout their body and energy field. Speak with confidence and be proud of your abilities.

18. Important: With your internal thoughts, ask your own healing guides to create a cleansing filter for you. Command that you bring all of you back to you, clean and clear. With your thoughts, pull any of your personal energy that might still be connected with the client back through the cleansing filter. Feel that all of you has returned to you.

YOUR MOMENT OF

Self-Awareness

Notice whatever you are thinking or feeling about these steps for intuitive Reiki. Are they different or are they similar to what you are already doing? Does it feel right to you? Practice all the steps now with someone at a distance. Write down the instant details of your awareness.

_____

_____

_____

_____

_____

_____

_____

_____

_____

_____

_____

_____

_____

_____

_____

_____

_____

CHAPTER 8

The Non-Physical Realm Is Real

I want you to be educated and aware that the non-physical realm is real, it is massive, and it has many more components than the earth plane. I want you to be aware so you will not be surprised when you encounter its diversity.

The intuitive Reiki healer not only focuses on the physical body, but also the mind, the emotions, and the eternal soul. We receive information about a person's current story, their body, their energy field, and their eternal story. We begin to see how their current life and their past lives are affecting their well-being. We perceive someone's secrets, emotions, fears, and struggles. We find their beliefs, hidden pain, hidden joys, agony, but also their future potential and possibilities. We will know some of the hidden aspects of the person's illness, the patterns, complex relationships, emotional strife and illness within their bodies. We discover the ugly, the weird, the deeply private, and the sacred.

The intuitive Reiki practitioner must be compassionate, confidential, and without judgment. This is why we must always ask for permission either intuitively or in person. When you begin a Reiki session you are taking a physical, mental, emotional, and spiritual journey with that person.

The power of Reiki is often so strong that strange and sometimes scary things happen during a session. Sometimes new practitioners stop offering sessions because they do not know what is happening. Some have informed me that they had no idea their intuitive skills would explode. Some are so bombarded with intuitive information that they are overwhelmed and hesitate to continue to be a Reiki practitioner. I do not want you to stop because you struggle to understand the depth to which your Reiki healing will take you. I want you to take charge and trust what you receive and share that information with your clients. I hope to take the fear out of it with this open discussion and other people sharing their stories with you.

You will have surprising experiences with the non-physical realms because Reiki opened that doorway for you. We are not separate from the non-physical. We humans are physical and non-physical at the same time. Just like our physical world, there is negative and positive in the non-physical realm. I have had the room fill up with blinding light and within the light stood a stunning archangel giving my client a message. Dark clouds of black have lifted up and out of my client's heart. I have witnessed very negative deceased people interfering with my client's life and watched as Reiki lifted them away. Sometimes the room filled up with my client's deceased loved ones sending encouragement and love.

Angels have bent over and kissed my client on the forehead or placed their own hands on my client's body. Reiki reveals the full spectrum of life to you. There is no need to fear. My book *Advanced Medical Intuition* addresses the non-physical realms of life in great detail.

Here are four Reiki healers who have decided to share some of their non-physical experiences and want to help you understand and trust your abilities.

Personal Story: Cara Gallucci

From time to time, people have reported feeling invisible presences during Reiki sessions. Not uncommonly, clients will tell me that even though they knew there was no one else in the room with us, they felt a second set of hands on their bodies along with my own. Or they may say that even when they felt my hands moving to a new position, they could still feel my hands working at the previous position as well. In one instance, a client at our Reiki clinic shared with me that he had been struggling for a long time to feel connected to God. He considered himself an agnostic with only an intellectual idea of what God might be. At the end of our session, he let me know that for the first time in his life, he had felt the presence of God in the room while several of us were administering Reiki at our respective tables. What a beautiful affirmation that it is not our own energy we use when we give Reiki, but something great and mysterious that flows through us.

Cara Gallucci
www.OmniStressRelief.com
781-724-2982

Personal Story: Anonymous

This Reiki practitioner wants you to know there are really no boundaries in the energetic realm. I included this story to help you see that we healers are working in a very complicated multidimensional cosmos. Reiki's high level of energy opens those worlds to us. There is no reason to be afraid. There is every reason to rejoice and be a more active participant in all the realms of healing.

I had an incredible experience that I wanted to share. I listen to emotionally motivating music at night. I find film scores the best, like the music in Gladiator, Last of the Mohicans, Brave Heart etc. For the duration [of a distant healing session] I close my eyes, with the music playing for five to eight minutes. I pour my soul into healing that person. I get so involved. I whisper what I'm doing so the Universe knows what I'm seeing and doing.

I move my hands like the conductor of an orchestra. Sometimes their skin comes off. I'm looking at muscles, organs. I heal every bit I see. It's all red. I can't see any colors, just red, like meat, or dark red, browns. I massage, move my hands across the body, remove chalk, brown bits. Darkness comes away, flesh is lighter and clear.

Then their skin comes back on and I can see their energy. Beautiful colors then shoot through the body. The healing moves from the physical to ethereal levels. Then comes silver, white, golds.

The song then ends. The most amazing healings in those minutes. When I open my eyes, it is like coming out of a trance, and I'm so awake and alive.

One night I did it to myself. I imagined I was approaching myself lying on a bed. I had dark crap in my arteries, stomach, chalk in my veins, dust in my lungs. It all got removed and pushed out. Polyps on my throat were removed. Then my skin was put back on. Colors came, the chakras shone. As each one popped with so much color starting from my crown, I could feel it in my physical body. Like a warm heat moving through. Amazing.

Beautiful rainbows in clear white light swirled, dancing to the music. I then saw a lotus in my head. It was closed. The petals opened and I saw my pineal, a hard, white rosebud, encased in white glass-like egg shell stuff. The white rosebud shook with vibration and the hard stuff shattered off it.

Then I was dancing to the music on a massive white disc, like doing modern ballet. I was on a stage, dancing on this disc suspended in midair. My opponent was a dark mass. I pushed, punched, and kicked (all to dance movement with love in my heart). With balls of white swirling energy in my hands, I danced the winning fight against the dark force of the Universe until my opponent diminished and was no more. Angels then stood and clapped. My song then ended.

Anonymous

Personal Story: Jennifer Allgier

When I first started practicing Reiki on humans, I followed the hand positions I had in my classes. Sometimes I was aware of energy flowing from me and sometimes not. After a while, I became aware of hearing messages: "Treat the eyes." "Her shoulder hurts." "She doesn't like that." That sort of thing. Sometimes I was aware of spirit presences when I was doing Reiki. Sometimes I felt my hands being pushed or pulled to certain areas of a person's body. This is still disconcerting and puzzling to me when it happens, I guess because I'm not sure who is doing the pushing. As I have become more willing to listen and allow myself to be guided, I have become more intuitive in my treatments and have more trust that the outcomes will be what are truly needed.

The experience that drew me to begin to study medical intuition occurred a year or two after I started practicing Reiki. I was giving a treatment to my husband. The room was dimly lit. I became aware of a blue-white glow surrounding his body. I suddenly realized I was seeing through my husband's skin to the bones of his skull. This was really weird, but I trusted the Reiki and kept on. I felt drawn to a foramen over the upper left side of his mouth, above the teeth and below the eye. I remember I couldn't keep from staring at it. I heard, "His teeth hurt." I sent Reiki to this area for a long time.

I then felt drawn to an area a bit higher than the stomach, between the heart chakra and the solar plexus. I was still very aware that I was seeing into my husband's body, and I tried not to look back at his skull. (I mean, you know, it was my husband's *skull*!) If I had stopped at that point to think about this or allowed myself to be freaked out, then I couldn't have continued giving Reiki.

My husband looked sort of like one of those plastic see-through anatomy models—the plastic covering was the blue-white light. As I treated the area above his stomach, I observed something rising out of his body from between the heart chakra and diaphragm. It was transparent and grayish-white in color and appeared to have sort of a skull-like "head" with trailing wispy parts. I kept giving Reiki. It is sort of a rule of mine: When in doubt, do Reiki. The entity disappeared. I finished the treatment.

Afterwards, I asked my husband how he felt. He is not at all versed in Reiki and is pretty skeptical about anything other than "ordinary" physical reality. He said he felt good, like he had "really released something." I didn't tell him what I saw because I did not want to frighten him. Honestly, I was a bit frightened. I kept thinking, "What *was* that?" I asked him if his teeth hurt. I remember him saying they didn't, but very shortly afterwards he was diagnosed with periodontal disease in the area I had been directed to. He required only one laser treatment from his dentist. In retrospect, I understand that the foramen I kept staring at is the infraorbital foramen. It's an opening where part of the maxillary nerve emerges from the skull. This nerve receives sensory information from the teeth.

Also, around the same time, my husband was admitted to the ER with what we thought was a heart attack but thankfully turned out to be acid reflux secondary to Helicobacter. I gave more Reiki at the time of the ER visit, but I wish I had been proactive and discussed what I had seen in the upper stomach area. It was many months later that I learned other people had similar experiences and that one could learn techniques to facilitate such visualization.

Reiki has been moving me toward embracing the intuitive parts of myself. It is fair to say I am now seeing life more from a spiritual standpoint. I feel more connected to the essence of Spirit that flows throughout creation. I'm more accepting of what life teaches and have greater understanding that I am here on earth as both learner and teacher. I worry less (believe me, I was very good at it) and have greater peace. With conventional Western veterinary medicine and now herbal medicine, I attempt to remove physical impediments to wellness and assist an individual's body in healing. With Reiki, I offer assistance to the individual's life force and spirit that can be used in creating wholeness. Medical intuition brings insight that can help focus both physical medicine and energy work for the "highest good."

Jenny Allgier
minusan@aol.com

Jenny boldly shared her healing story. For some of you, the experience she had witnessing a being release from her husband will seem farfetched and impossible. For others, you might be relieved to know that someone else has had these strange and sometimes scary experiences during a healing session. Yes, this was a real healing event. And yes, the more you allow love to flow through you, the more your clients will release all kinds of negativity.

Personal Story: Elise Mori

The first time I did a Reiki healing in exchange for money, I was so nervous because the woman I was healing was very cool, and I really wanted to impress her. I live in Japan, and my client lived about a five-minute walk away from Tokyo Sky Tree, which is so tall I can barely bring myself even to look at it.

What happened was that I impressed myself with my clairvoyance, which I had no idea I had until then. I saw the spirit and healing guides of the person, as well as my own healing guides, come into the room and heal her alongside me. The client had a lot of very serious problems with her parents, and during the Reiki session something very deeply shifted for her. You could see the transformation in her face. As I left her apartment and walked down the street, I could actually see the glowing, shimmering presences making a circle with me in a healing team, and then slowly part and go their own ways. It was the most magical experience I had had to date, and I have been a ritual magic practitioner for many years.

Since then, I've had some incredible moments, one involving the god Anubis and a sapphire, another with some giant spiders, and another with a blue jelly-like individual. I think the way Reiki has influenced my intuition is in guiding me towards teachers, all of whom have helped me to understand how to access my intuition and build it up from basically nothing, like a muscle. Because Reiki is so perfect, it helps you to empower yourself and learn and grow at your own speed through self-inquiry and self-development, which is of course the very best way.

Because of Reiki, the impact it has had on my life, and the way it has guided me and indirectly taught me to be my own best resource, I no longer perform ritual magic, even though working with talismans, angels, and archangels has also catalyzed me to being where I am today. I am not saying that I am now some kind of super-sensory guru-like intuitive who can just look at someone and say what they had for breakfast a week ago last Tuesday, but certainly stuff is happening.

When I heal with Reiki, there isn't always some effect. Sometimes absolutely nothing at all happens. I think that's because the person doesn't want or need healing. It's not up to us to decide what or who needs healing. We can only give it our best shot and keep our fingers crossed. Sometimes, you actually see the effect, like the woman in Tokyo I described. I've also had success with instant healing of skin complaints and broken bones. But sometimes the effect is subtle. Maybe the person feels the need for some life direction changes. For example, a friend of mine had several sessions with me and it led her to have therapy, which was much more effective for her than Reiki. But, of course, I want to believe that it was the Reiki that caused her to get talk therapy! When I give healing, that's the kind of effect I like the best, I think.

Now I teach Reiki and that is such a huge blast. I love it. For me, the most important thing I teach my students is what Usui Sensei called "Anshin Ritsumei," or perfect peace of mind. Being and experiencing Reiki, and allowing it to spontaneously flow out from everything I do, is the biggest impact that Reiki has had on my life. Reiki's impact on me is beyond description or understanding. I thank God, and Usui Sensei, every day for bringing Reiki into my life, and I can't imagine not having Reiki in my life.

Elise Mori

www.lotusforest.net

YOUR MOMENT OF

Self-Awareness

Be completely honest with yourself. Can you recall events that leaped into your awareness during Reiki that seemed mysterious, astonishing, or even impossible? Did you push the event aside and completely doubt or discredit it as nonsense? Please allow yourself to explore it during this private time. Write down the instant details of your awareness.

_____

_____

_____

_____

_____

_____

_____

_____

_____

_____

CHAPTER 9

Intuitive Reiki with Animals

Many people who come to my workshop tell me that they do not plan to work with people because their focus is animals. Some say they are dog people and some say they are cat people and many want to assist all animals. It does not seem to matter the kind of animal when it comes to Reiki. I have, however, noticed a couple of differences with animals receiving energy work. They tend to walk away when they have received enough, usually within just a few minutes, while humans stretch out and soak it up for as long as you allow them to be there.

Animals do not carry as much baggage as we people carry. If an animal carries any emotions, your intuition will usually show you that they have soaked it up from emotional humans in the home. Animals in our homes tend to absorb and carry our burdens. It is often a huge weight for them to carry for us.

Reiki and intuition are exactly the same for animals and humans. Animals seem to telepathically send us a great deal of information about their struggles through images in our minds. They frequently communicate in images instead of words.

I have a fantastic example from my own life. My sweet cat Nicki became a nervous wreck. She began yowling loudly off and on most of the night, missing her litter box, and pacing all over the house. I was so emotional about her that I could not receive clear information from her. I reached out to an animal communicator for help.

I waited and a few days later the animal communicator got back to me. She said that all she could perceive was a giant aquarium with a large snake weaving back and forth in it. She described Nicki feeling a great deal of fear. She apologized for failing me and failing Nicki. I was astounded and quickly informed her that my family member loves snakes and he recently purchased one with a giant tank and placed it in the kitchen!

Besides being an example of how Nicki showed the animal communicator an image, this is also one of the most perfect examples of how intuitives frequently convince themselves they are failing when in fact they are perfectly correct. The intuitive animal communicator decided she was failing both Nicki and me because she could not interpret or make sense of what she received. Notice the difference if this intuitive would have simply said to me, "All Nicki keeps showing me is a huge snake weaving back and forth in a huge aquarium. She feels terrified. Does that make any sense to you?" She would not try to make any sense of it and she would completely trust what she received, no matter what it was. Oh, and if you are wondering what happened, the snake went to a very good home where there were no cats to terrify.

One more point I want to make. We will never be the clearest when we are emotional. I was emotional about my cat and was unable to receive intuitive information to help her out. Emotion will always get in our way. It will not matter if we are emotional about our animals or the humans we care about. Emotion clogs up the clear flow of Reiki and of intuition.

Personal Story: Jennifer Allgier

In Chapter 8, Jennifer shared about her intuitive Reiki experiences with her husband, and now she shares her animal stories as well as how Reiki rebuilt herself and her career as a veterinarian.

I was introduced to Reiki five years ago. It has changed, no, it has *transformed* my life. I am now a Holy Fire II Karuna and Usui Reiki master. I do not currently practice professionally. I do participate in a monthly Reiki share that is open to the public. I am a veterinarian in my "ordinary" life, and I offer Reiki informally to my patients when there is opportunity to do so. It has helped my patients directly, has brought me greater intuitive understanding of how to treat them medically, and has given me greater understanding and acceptance of spiritual help in general.

There have been ill and injured animals I was sure would not survive that then made recoveries that could only be called miraculous after receiving Reiki: a cat with recurrent urethral obstruction, a dog in renal failure, a septic cat with a ruptured uterus . . .

I have also reached out to animals with distant Reiki and realized that the patient had moved beyond my reach and was in the process of passing on to its next life. The Reiki sent then was with the intent that the transition be smooth and easy. I have seen the spirits of animals as they are leaving this life. One was my own beloved dog, Willow. They appear to have guides much as we do. Their spirits seem large, much larger than their small animal bodies.

Reiki has given me greater faith that everything isn't (and isn't supposed to be) up to me to fix, and that sometimes the highest good isn't what I personally might think it should be. Most practitioners say a sort of prayer before a Reiki treatment, asking that their egos step aside and that the Reiki energies work for the highest good. We also ask for permission to treat, even from animals. Reiki is only helpful if an individual wants to receive it.

I was a very conventional veterinarian before receiving Reiki. Thinking back on my life, there was often spiritual help, but I tended to discount it as not real. I am at a point where I can no longer practice or, for that matter, live as I used to. Having had my conventional beliefs disrupted, I am rebuilding both self and career.

Jennifer Allgier
minusan@aol.com

Personal Story: Julie Rebensdorf, MA, LSW

My involvement with Reiki began in my younger years. My degree in psychology wasn't enough to satisfy an urgent calling within me. I delved into metaphysics for a number of years, learning about meditation and Eastern religious philosophy, where I became interested in nontraditional forms of healing. I went on to receive a master's degree in counseling, and an LSW, or Licensure in Social Work, which brought me closer to my core, but was still not enough. During this time, I began studying and working with Reiki while helping others in my social work specialty of Alzheimer's.

It didn't take long to find that Reiki was where I really connected with my inner soul. It utilized both my physical study of bodily energies and my metaphysical development of intuition. I continued doing Reiki in my free time, even with my pets. I began to see how it worked on animals as well as humans. I kept up with my daily meditations and noticed I could sense where a problem was on an animal without their input. Over the years I have had some remarkable experiences with both humans and animals.

I would like to share one story about an animal that is so simple, yet so powerful and true. I was asked by a good friend to work on one of her husband's horses. Since they lived a good deal away from me, it was going to be a long-distance Reiki session. My friend's husband taught polo and was very knowledgeable about horses. However, he could not figure out what was wrong with one mare named Do Re Me. The horse was giving him a difficult time. That's all the background information I received.

As I meditated and did my long-distance Reiki over the horse's body, I listened to my higher self and intuition. I could find nothing physically wrong with the horse. All I could see in my mind's eye was Do Re Me stomping at the ground in aggravation. Although it didn't seem like much, I reported this to my friend, only to find that Do Re Me was doing just that! Apparently, my friend's husband was teaching the horse a series of movements that included putting her head down, then picking up her hoof and pawing the ground, concluding with the horse lying on the ground. Do Re Me had done this series many times before and already knew it well.

Horses have their own body language. For example, it's natural for horses to paw the ground when they are tired or bored. They will stomp the ground when irritated. Do Re Me was using horse language, and a bit of horse emotion, to tell him she already knew this series of movements. Enough already!

Julie Rebensdorf, MA, LSW
julierebensdorf@yahoo.com

YOUR MOMENT OF

Self-Awareness

Have you offered Reiki to animals? If not, please do so. Notice intuitive information that popped in. Was it similar to your intuition with humans or different? Did you discount or push it aside? Write down the instant details of your awareness.

Part Two

A Union of Healing and Wisdom

CHAPTER 10

Your Intuitive Wisdom of the Reiki Symbols

When a system, an organization, or an individual has secrets, the only one who benefits is the one who knows the secrets. Secrets are for control and holding onto power. I personally feel that we are in a time of expansion with profound gateways opening wide. The ancient Reiki symbols used to be top secret. These symbols set Reiki apart from other energy modalities. The old symbols have come from the ancient histories of Japan, Tibet, and India. Now all kinds and versions of new symbols have recently been created by current-day Reiki masters.

Diane Stein was the first that I am aware of who placed the symbols in her book for all to see. I think I was the second person to place the symbols into print in my book *The Reiki Teacher's Manual*. I will not hold onto secrets in order to feel more powerful or to have more control. I did not hold on to the secret symbols in the past, and I do not keep secrets from the students who attend my medical intuitive workshop now. I tell everything I know and everything I have witnessed or experienced. Even now, I am not holding back in this book. I especially want people to understand that intuition does have an honored place in a Reiki healing. Intuition can always be ignored, but it can never be separate from Reiki.

As I said earlier, Spirit often speaks to us with symbolic images. Symbols are an efficient way to provide a lot of information. We quickly intuit a brief story from a symbol. Most people would say that Reiki symbols are really not symbols because they are just black lines on a piece of paper. The symbols are so much more than that. These symbols represent certain aspects of healing. Tens of thousands of people have looked at them, felt them, and utilized them in their healing sessions.

Symbols are all around us. A photo of someone represents that split second in his or her life. A piece of jewelry, a watch, a ring, or any belonging that was loved by someone is also a symbol. Human energy imprints into objects. Psychometry is the ability to receive intuitive information about a person from an object that belonged to them. Intuitives can discern this information because our human energy is so powerful. Religious symbols such as the Christian cross, the Buddhist dharma wheel, and Islam's crescent and star are only a few examples of the intense importance of symbols. They each hold all the feelings, emotions, thoughts, and prayers of all individuals who have looked at or have held the symbols. Human energy is deeply entrenched in symbols.

The Reiki symbols are also deeply imprinted with energy. They are keys, or triggers, that activate a higher, more refined energy transference. Each symbol carries its own vibration, meaning, and function. Each sacred symbol escalates the intensity of the electrical vibration it represents. The symbols do not activate themselves. They are activated during the attunement when the master-teacher energetically draws them into the person's energy field. Drawing them into someone's field literally embeds them in the receiver's life force. Each time a student achieves the next level or degree of Reiki, those symbols are imprinted again into the person's energy field. Each time the symbols are imprinted, the connection between human and Reiki strengthens. The symbols become more and more of who we are. As time goes on a natural harmony between human and symbol develops and blends together.

Although our hands send very focused energy, the sacred symbols do not stay in our hands alone. Our entire being becomes a Reiki being, and the symbols radiate throughout our essence. Your energy mingles with the energy of the symbols and vice versa. We literally emit Reiki in all directions twenty-four hours a day. Let the symbols speak to you. Stop for a moment and consider each symbol. Do you feel that special connection with one or two of them more than the others? Has the familiarity with some of the symbols remained the same or has there been changes over time?

Because our thoughts are so tremendously powerful, I am convinced that working deliberately with clear, direct intent and also feeling the symbols generates a more precise channel through the practitioner. When one of the symbols leaps into your awareness during a session, focus on it with all your love. Then imagine opening your entire being as a vessel for it to flow through you. Your energy co-mingles with the power of the symbols, causing its true vibration to flourish. When you merge your own conscious intent with each particular symbol, the healings will intensify exponentially. Your intense connected feeling about a symbol assists the focus that it already holds. You become a team with the ancient symbols.

For example, the Sei He Kei focuses on clearing and cleansing. If you have an affinity for this symbol, the energy of cleansing will be even more profound as you use it. Your intensity and focus accentuate the symbol's focus. As a Reiki practitioner, you link together in a synchronized manner with the Sei He Kei for the best clearing and cleansing possible.

I have also noticed over the years that occasionally the symbols alter themselves in some way while working with certain clients with certain illnesses, diseases, or life conditions. For example, the symbols might have begun as its name in my mind and then appear visually in my mind's eye. Or I could see the symbol with open eyes and it seemed to sit on top of an individual's skin. Sometimes the symbol would begin by sitting on the skin, then sinking down into the individual's body and deep into an organ or a bone, etc. The black lines of a symbol might suddenly or slowly change to a color. (Please know that colors are specific vibrations of energy and also specific information. For more information regarding color, see Chapter 12.)

As you use the symbols, you will have thoughts and feelings for each one. You will recognize that each one is so very different. Feeling each one of them is very important. I ask that you develop a personal relationship with them. As you work with the symbols, you can use them in various ways. There is no right or wrong way. Use them and feel the surge of a more powerful energy. Use them consciously and with clear intent. Remember, all the symbols can be used for humans, animals, plants, intersections of roads with high death rates, our past traumas, our automobiles, our washing machines, our sleep time, our homes, our workplace, our earth, and our Universe. This is a mere fraction of uses for Reiki, but I hope it expands your thoughts about using it daily and using it everywhere and anywhere.

I will now cover the traditional symbols and ask you to notice certain characteristics and certain values with each of them. At the end of intuitively sensing the five traditional symbols in this section, I will ask you to repeat these same steps for any other symbols you have been taught to use. I ask that you allow yourself to intuitively compare the old and the newer symbols in a nonjudgmental manner. Get to know and understand what is really happening when you focus on them and what you become aware of.

Let us now discuss each symbol. Linger upon each one so you can intuitively perceive more information and create a deeper connection with it.

Sei He Kei

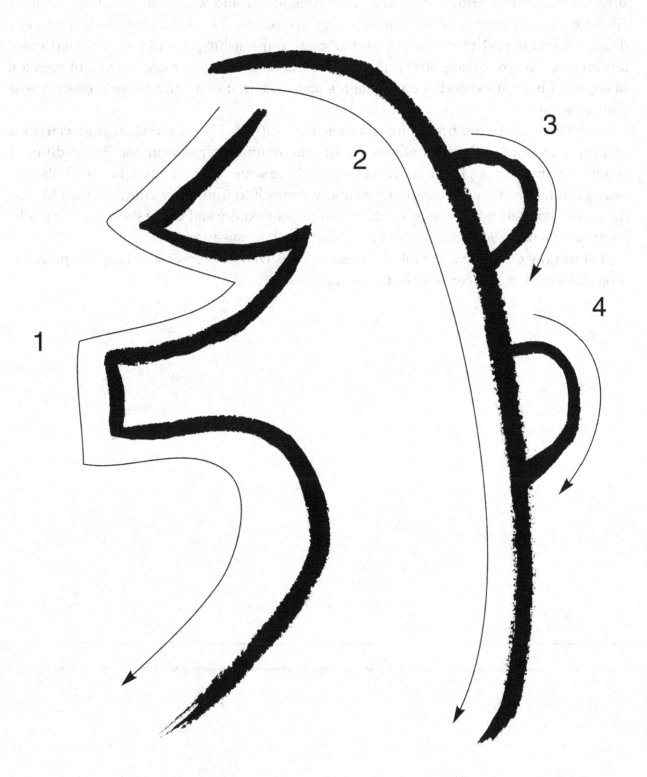

Let's begin with this symbol because of what it is about. This symbol is based in Japanese history and culture. The Sei He Kei clears and cleanses. What is also interesting is the symbol vibrates in the emotional realm. When you consider the whole spectrum of human emotions, that might begin to make sense. Emotions are real "things." Earlier, we talked about suffering, fear, shame, and other emotions that have slow, sluggish, and constrictive energies. That density can lead to physical and mental illness. Illness originates from old hurts, anguish, disappointment, shame, or stuck emotions. The Sei He Kei breaks up the dense qualities of negative emotions to be lifted away.

This symbol transforms the negative into the positive. To live in a healthy state, we must allow our emotions to move and flow. The Sei He Kei brings the heaviness of life up and out for release. It will bring forth that which we have suppressed and ignored into our conscious awareness so we can learn and then release. I use this symbol nearly all the time because some type or level of emotion is always present as illness develops. When someone says "Lighten up!" this is the symbol to help do that very thing.

The Sei He Kei is also used to clear anything and everything. For example, has there been chronic conflict in your work place? Cleanse and clear out the heaviness that is interfering with the progress that everyone wants to have. Animals absorb our thoughts and emotions, especially those animals who have chosen to dwell with humans. Please use the Sei He Kei with them. Animals will not allow an hour-long session. They are not as dense as humans are, so only a few minutes is usually required. They will let you know. Your hands do not even need to lie still on them. Send the Sei He Kei deep inside while you stroke them in the manner that they are accustomed to. Send it from your whole body while they lie in your lap. You will find that cats especially are "Reiki junkies." Your cat will be right at your side when you offer Reiki in your home.

The Sei He Kei lifts and refines heavy, dense vibrations into a finer, higher frequency of the positive. Use it in house clearings of negative energy where fighting or agitated arguments keep happening. Use it when something terrible has happened in a home or building or on the property. Use it for struggling relationships or food cooked at home or a restaurant.

I have noticed that the Sei He Kei seems to be the least altered symbol. That is to say, it seems the most consistent of all the symbols and appears nearly the same everywhere. I think I use the Sei He Kei more than any other symbol. Actively use it for yourself, your clients, and in any other way you can think of, and you will notice the difference.

YOUR MOMENT OF

Self-Awareness

Place the image of the Sei He Kei in front of you. Whisper its name. Envision yourself going deep into the inner recesses of this symbol, immersing yourself in it, aware that each symbol feels different and each symbol moves in its own perfect dance. Write down the instant details of your awareness.

_____

_____

_____

_____

_____

_____

_____

_____

_____

_____

Cho Ku Rei

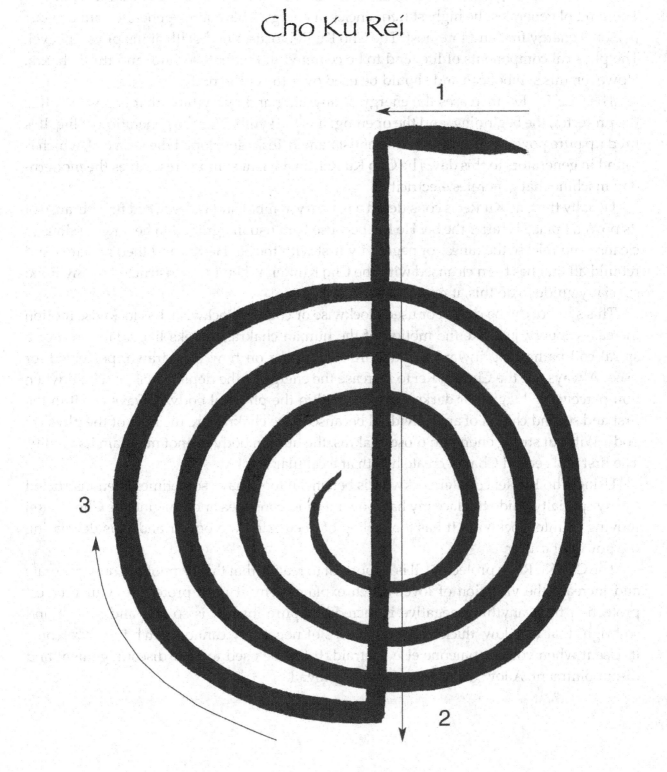

The Cho Ku Rei originates from the land of Tibet. It vibrates on the physical level of life. The symbol generates the highest frequencies of energy. This energy generator builds your personal energy first and foremost. The Cho Ku Rei focuses on health at the physical level. The physical components of life tend to be centered in the first, second, and third chakra. However, this symbol can and should be used over the entire body.

The Cho Ku Rei increases the energy of anything and everything that is positive. It is the protector, the beginning, and the opening. It is the symbol for the generation of life. It is fired up pure power as it turns on. A scientist named Tesla developed the tesla coil, which is found in generators to this day. The Cho Ku Rei, an ancient symbol, resembles the modern-day machine that generates electricity!

Usually the Cho Ku Rei is considered a primary symbol and is described first because of its power. I placed it after the Sei He Kei because I am usually guided in healing sessions to cleanse and release the illness or negativity first with the Sei He Kei and then recharge and rebuild all that has been cleansed with the Cho Ku Rei. When I was instructed by my Reiki specialty guide to do this, it made so much sense.

This symbol can be drawn or used clockwise or counterclockwise. Its clockwise motion increases energy, just like the motion of the human chakra. It looks like a labyrinth or a spiral coil path going inward or outward depending on how it is drawn, perceived, or used. Always use the Cho Ku Rei to increase the energy of the depleted client. Use it when you perceive a sluggish or darkened place within the physical body. Always use it in the first and second chakra of an individual because those chakras are the base of the physical body. Without strong energy in those chakras, the human body cannot maintain its vitality. The first and second Chakra create health at a cellular level.

Using Cho Ku Rei counterclockwise is beneficial too. I have sometimes been instructed by my specialty guide to place my hand over a cancerous area and imagine the Cho Ku Rei moving counterclockwise. It has the feeling of decreasing the power and thus decreasing the power of cancer.

The Cho Ku Rei is protective. It is important to realize that this symbol can only generate and increase the vibration of love, which explains why it is so protective. Our greatest protection from anything negative is incredible, pure love. It is so fine and so fast and so bright that the slow, thickened frequencies of negativity cannot match it or overcome it. Use it when you or someone else is afraid. It can be used to alter discouragement and disappointment. Allow the power of love to prevail.

YOUR MOMENT OF

Self-Awareness

Place the image of the Cho Ku Rei in front of you. Whisper its name. Envision yourself going deep into the inner recesses of this symbol, immersing yourself in it, aware that each symbol feels different and each symbol moves in its own perfect dance. Write down the instant details of your awareness.

Hon Sha Ze Sho Nen

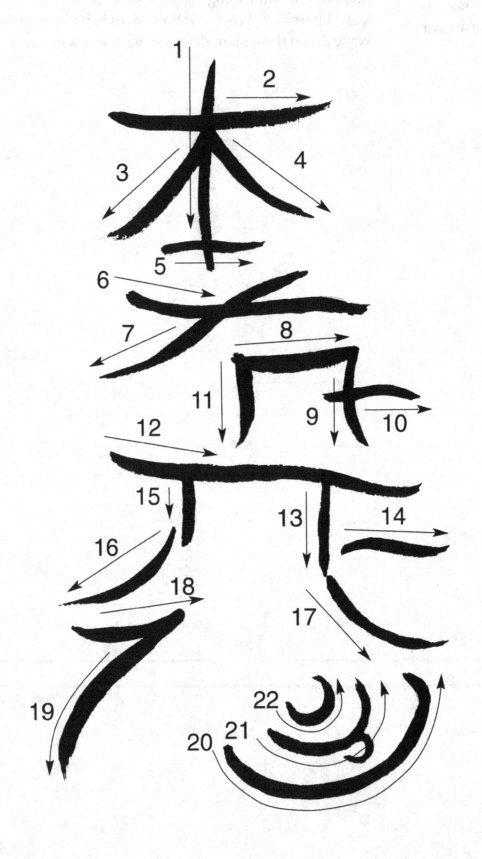

The Hon Sha Ze Sho Nen originated in Japan. I love this symbol because of the mind-expanding service it does for us. Some might tell you that its true function is impossible. The Hon Sha Ze Sho Nen literally means "No past, no present, no future." That might still seem vague. Its frequency vibrates without any limits. It is limitless. The Universe has no limits and neither does its abilities. Non-physical realms of life are timeless and unobstructed. This symbol gives access to send healing to the past, to the present, and to all the potential of the future. This symbol heightens our intuition by expanding our awareness beyond old constraints. For a moment allow your mind to contemplate an unlimited system of infinite intelligence.

Time is not limited by the constraints that we humans created in order to measure it. We try to understand time by creating calendars and clocks. Measuring time helps us stay on track in our everyday lives, but it is an elementary way to comprehend it. Time does not limit energy and neither does distance. Energy never dwindles across time, space, or distance. Reiki healings also do not dwindle across time or space. Reiki does not lose its power even when sent to someone on the other side of the world. It arrives instantly, just as powerful as when you initially sent it.

The Hon Sha Ze Sho Nen enhances and enriches the healing aspect of Reiki across time, distance, and space. It allows us to program the beat or the electrical rhythm across any distance to the receiver. In other words, you can set your intent for the healing pulsations to replicate within any time frame that you choose. For example, during an emergency, one might set the intent with this symbol for Reiki to go to the individual every minute for the next eight hours. Another example might be sending Reiki to a friend who is terribly frightened of getting on an airplane. You can send Reiki to them and the plane for two hours on that day, one hour before the flight, and during the flight.

Remember, these are only examples. Ask your Reiki specialist what vibrational pulsing feels the best for any given situation. Specifically ask your specialist for the optimal healing frequency and optimal rate to send the healing, and it will be there. Again, when we specifically call out to our most holy and sacred Reiki specialty guide for assistance, please remember to accept the first thing that comes into your mind. Do not accept the second or third idea that leaps in. Accept only the first leaping thought.

Time does not only move forward but exists in all directions. All time is now. Our past moments in our current life and our past moments in our past lives are just as relevant and just as accessible. We humans can send Reiki healing into our own younger years and we can send Reiki into our own past lives. We can do this for ourselves and we are capable of doing this for the people we are giving Reiki to.

Using the Hon Sha Ze Sho Nen, send Reiki to a personal past moment that has remained painful to you. It does not matter the situation or the level of pain around that moment. It can be healed and released today. If you think it will take a long time, then it will. If you are convinced that it can be done now, it can be done now.

Learning this symbol is daunting to most people. So here is how I memorized it. Notice that there are five segments making up this symbol as well as five parts that make up its name: Hon Sha Ze Sho Nen. Connect the symbol's segments with portions of its name. So, the top portion of the symbol would represent Hon, the second portion would be Sha and so on.

You can draw the symbol on paper to learn it, but I finally had to do something else. I stood up and drew it in the air. As I drew it in the air, I began to feel myself moving. It began to feel like a graceful dance. I quickly loved this symbol and was able to memorize it easily. Get a sense of the dance as you draw it. The dance will take away the worry about its complexity. With a smile on your face, stand up and dance with it.

YOUR MOMENT OF

Self-Awareness

Place the image of the Hon Sha Ze Sho Nen in front of you. Whisper its name. Envision yourself going deep into the inner recesses of this symbol, immersing yourself in it, aware that each symbol feels different and each symbol moves in its own perfect dance. Write down the instant details of your awareness.

Dai Ko Myo

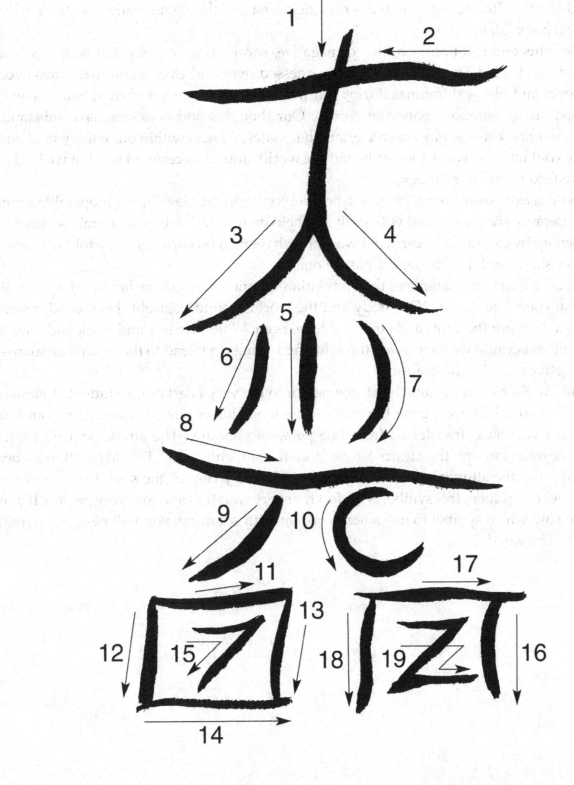

This symbol originated in Tibet. It vibrates right to the heart of one's soul. By using the Dai Ko Myo, you are virtually going to the very source of the illness or disease. It vibrates beyond the mundane physical world and alters the origin of the discomfort and illness. Basically, its healing vibration travels to the cause of an illness or struggle. Remember that the source of illness is not the physical body. Illness in the physical body is the result of something else. Illness begins in the energy field first and then potentially manifests in the physical body later on.

Thoughts and emotions, positive or negative, show up in our physical body because the body and mind are one unit. I have witnessed over and over again that unresolved emotional and physical traumas during our past lives influence our current body as well. The body-mind-emotion connection is real. Our thoughts and emotions have substance and matter and become physical material. That material floats within our energy field and radiates out into the world. Our body and the world around us respond to what we feed it, and we feed it with our thoughts.

I witnessed a dear loving person, who everyone adored, develop an inoperable brain tumor because she was racked with guilt and held on to a dark secret. Her brain seemed to be eaten up by the guilt she carried. I was the only person on earth who she told the secret to. After she shared it with me, she passed on.

This is a dramatic example of the body-mind-emotion connection, but the story is real, and that connection is real. Our body and the world around us, right this second, reflect exactly where our thoughts and emotions have been. Where we live and work and who is in our life is because we have given thought and feelings that lead to their manifestation— the negative and also the beautiful.

The Dai Ko Myo transmits the attunement into the very heart of the student. A similar example would be how a gene transmits to us the color of our eyes and hair from our parents. That trait is transferred from one person to another. The attunement transmits energetic traits through the master-teacher into the student. The Dai Ko Myo, all the other symbols, and the attunements are broadcast to the very core of the soul. Because of the heart-soul connection, this symbol is perfect for every situation and for every person. If you are not sure which symbol to use when working with someone, you will never go wrong with the Dai Ko Myo.

YOUR MOMENT OF

Self-Awareness

Place the image of the Dai Ko Myo in front of you. Whisper its name. Envision yourself going deep into the inner recesses of this symbol, immersing yourself in it, aware that each symbol feels different and each symbol moves in its own perfect dance. Write down the instant details of your awareness.

_____

_____

_____

_____

_____

_____

_____

_____

_____

_____

_____

Raku

The Raku is a mighty bolt of the finest, fastest, and most illuminating electrical force on earth. It is the commanding, electrical, fine-tuned frequency of love. The Raku is about true enlightenment and not meant to be a healing symbol. This lightning bolt symbol brings vivid aliveness through the attunement and down into the person's body. The lightning bolt binds, seals, and grounds the illumination within the client as much as the dense human body can tolerate. It also imprints the symbols into the spine and seals it with its jolt of energy. In this way, our entire human form emanates the Reiki frequency through every cell of our being. The Raku completes the circuitry by grounding the symbols and the attunement into the body, while at the same time disconnecting the master-teacher from the student's energy field instantly.

Raku is the lightning bolt linkage connecting heaven and earth. It is a passage, bridging the non-physical realm with the physical you. Allow the sacred ethereal energy of heaven to touch the earthly you in this moment. This is another reason why intuition and Reiki create a sacred union of healing and wisdom.

YOUR MOMENT OF

Self-Awareness

Place the image of the Raku in front of you. Whisper its name. Envision yourself going deep into the inner recesses of this symbol, immersing yourself in it, aware that each symbol feels different and each symbol moves in its own perfect dance. Write down the instant details of your awareness.

_____

_____

_____

_____

_____

_____

_____

_____

_____

_____

_____

Other Symbols

As I mentioned earlier, I now ask you to repeat these same steps for other symbols you are drawn to or have already worked with. I ask that you allow yourself to intuitively compare the old and the newer symbols in a nonjudgmental manner. Get to know and understand what is really happening when you focus on them. What do you become aware of?

YOUR MOMENT OF

Self-Awareness

Place the image of any other symbol you are using in front of you. Whisper its name. Envision yourself going deep into the inner recesses of this symbol, immersing yourself in it, aware that each symbol feels different and each symbol moves in its own perfect dance. Write down the instant details of your awareness.

_____

_____

_____

_____

_____

_____

CHAPTER 11

Your Intuitive Wisdom of the Three Degrees

The Reiki practitioner has the opportunity to take one, two, or three degrees or levels of training. Some practitioners choose to practice with only the first-degree training while others choose to advance to the third degree. Briefly, the first degree focuses on healing on the physical level. The new practitioner is asked to focus on their personal healing as well as offering Reiki sessions to others. The second degree focuses on mental and emotional healing. The third degree provides two phases: first, healing of the soul, and second, learning to teach Reiki and the attunements to students. This chapter addresses each degree and includes personal stories from those who took one, two, or three degrees.

Personal Story: Donna Parsons

I've heard about Reiki over the years and was always curious to experience it for myself. I did some research and decided to register for a class. Little did I know that I was in for something that would change my life forever. I remember the day of the class like it was yesterday. I went to the class and the teacher was talking about the different symbols. I sat there wondering what effect they could possibly have on me. After the lecture I had my Reiki attunement. While I was receiving it, I did not feel any strange sensation or energy running through my body like other people said they did. I felt normal. However, my experience was more profound than I could imagine.

The first thing that happened was my third eye opened within a week after the attunement, and I realized that I was seeing and feeling things that I had never seen or felt before. I started reading for my friends and families and could tell them things that were going to happen in the near future. I also realized I could see people, places, and events that weren't visible to the physical eyes. I started to search and grow on a higher spiritual level. Since then there has been a huge increase in my intuitive awareness and my spiritual abilities.

Donna Parsons
soulsurge9@gmail.com

Attunements

The attunements received after each level set Reiki apart from all other healing techniques. Attunements do not give you anything new that you didn't already have. They offer a sacred moment, an initiation, or a memorable crossing from one time of life into another. You are given a release of old burdens as the sacred symbols enter into you. The attunement heightens and strengthens your energy field to the cleanest, brightest vibration possible for you at that time. The first attunement charges you up from a low-wattage bulb to high-voltage bulb! It is like clicking on the lamp and turning the three-way bulb from the first brightness up to the next brightness. It opens the vessel that you already are and allows more universal wisdom to flow through you.

We do not lose control during an attunement. When we receive an attunement, it is up to us to allow the attunement to enter into our body and energy field. When we do allow the energy to enter our essence, it begins to release blockages or density within the physical body as well as your life. Each attunement you receive chips away at the densities in your body and your life. The attunements will continue to chip away a little at a time until the restriction crumbles.

Reiki itself continues your personal healing. The more you give Reiki to yourself, the lighter your energy field becomes. You begin to sense, or feel on an energetic basis, and you no longer rely totally on the physical level of life. You are no longer dependent on just seeing, hearing or reading information about life to understand what is going on. You can allow yourself to notice and even trust intuitive information. All that and more begins to happen with the attunement. The attunement gives birth to a newer you. It blasts open your closed doorways. It gives birth to the healer you are meant to be.

First Degree Wisdom

The first degree is about healing the healer first. It concentrates on the physical body at the cellular. We must cleanse and heal ourselves first and foremost before the highest work can be done for others. Again, it is like turning on the light bulb, but it is also similar to putting the key into the lock and opening the door just a crack. You begin to notice a different awareness. You become aware of information you did not previously notice. The door cracked open to reveal a glimpse of the non-physical realms of life. The non-physical is just as alive as the physical realm.

The body, aura, and chakras have their first cleansing release. This first degree leads students to realize that Reiki is for everything—our animal friends, our food, plants, our homes, work places and even our cars. Reiki energy is truly for the good of all.

As you adjust to the attunement, it is imperative that you give Reiki to yourself daily, if only for a few minutes. This gives you the opportunity to cleanse and heal yourself but also to learn about the energy and to feel it more physically within you. It is then imperative that you give Reiki to people and everything around you. The more you use Reiki, the clearer, stronger, and more refined a Light Being you become.

Personal Story: Maryann Kelly

While volumes have been written about Reiki and its relationship to intuition, I am focusing specifically on Reiki Level I attunement and its subsequent twenty-one-day cleansing period when energy is moving through the chakra system. For me, this period was profound in further contributing to opening up my intuition. This Reiki attunement in combination with my weekly commitment to Light Grid sessions to collapse old belief systems, energy movement via dance, and continual practice performing client readings were the pivotal factors to my intuition further opening.

The further opening of my crown chakra to access and channel universal energy light and enable the flow of universal wisdom enhanced my ability to obtain and sustain a connection with either the direct client or with those passed over.

As my throat chakra opened further to enhance communications, my choice of words and phrases, both verbal and written, resonated and had improved meaning so that I could provide more of a positive and impactful experience for my client. The opening as well of the spinal column enabled me to become more grounded and anchored to keep the needed balance of grounding with my sustained higher vibrations.

With Level I's attunement, the associated enhanced energy flow resulted in a balancing of my right and left brain for clearer thinking and action. Consequently, doubt diminished and was replaced with justified conviction and confident commitment to action to benefit the client.

The further opening of the sixth and seventh chakras with their corresponding respective pineal and pituitary glands balanced my endocrine system, increased my perception of light, and connected me to a universal source of energy, which collectively increased higher consciousness, divine wisdom.

So, what does Reiki Level I attunement really mean to me in visceral, tangible, and practical terms as far as intuition? It has collectively meant that the spiritual mediumship readings I do to connect with loved ones, to obtain holistic health information, to remove cords, and/or to do past life regressions have markedly improved. I am more grounded, can viscerally feel more subtle changes in energy, and tangibly differentiate whether there are reactionary changes originating from internal client issues or external environmental factors, and I can more accurately and specifically interpret messages and information relayed via the language of energy or intuition.

The practical validation of the profound impact of this Reiki attunement on my application of intuition is that more clients are referred to me and more clients return. I am evidence of how integrating holistic complementary modalities such as Reiki with further opening of my intuition benefits the clients, the practitioner, and those interacting with the practitioner more casually on a daily basis.

The emphasis on the greater good is important as well. Intuition serves a purpose of good. Making Intuition Intentional[SM] is about empowering yourself and others to act with purpose aligned with positive intentions. Intuition is meant to serve you so that you can be your best self, define and respect boundaries regarding others and situations, and avoid the roles of perpetrator, victim, or rescuer. Intuition is not intended to support negativity, revenge, resentment, anger, etc., which ultimately serve no one and hurt many. A great upside about wanting to leverage your intuition is that you address your own issues in the process, which is healing and liberating. While addressing your own issues doesn't make life devoid of struggle and human emotion, doing real work on ourselves enables us to experience more joy, to be better able to navigate the challenges with fewer casualties personally or to others, and to expand the type of highs beyond what could have previously been imagined.

As my intuition expanded, more dots connected. In fact, I had an increasing realization of just how connected we all are. During moments being quiet, during readings with clients, and during moments of being present, I was grounded and calmly waited without anticipation as to what would be next. In such moments, time and space suspended. While the experience of suspension of time and space is not uncommon among those immersed in joy or other all-consuming situations, for me, it was when both new neural pathways were being formed (neuroplasticity) and when I was quiet and grounded and just waiting and listening with no control over the outcome (intuition) that the experience transcended time and space as defined by metaphysics.

Upon my realization of the factors involved enabling my intuition as described above, I was then able to further focus my determined will and adjust and reproduce that quiet state to amplify my intuition reception, so to speak. This quiet state was in stark contrast to decades of my past. As situations ebb and flow with countless variables and distractions, it is important to be able to shut out this noise to get into a quiet and calm place internally to access intuition for personal reasons or to serve a client.

As I realized more connectedness to a greater good, a corresponding sense of humility was also realized. Along with many others, I am very grateful to Tina Zion for her most unique and gifted way to teach medical intuition that inspires others to demonstrate abilities with conviction in service of others. In short, Reiki is a contributing catalyst fueling my intuition opening up and enabling me to be a better version of myself. While each has a unique experience, this is mine, and I hope it helps others.

Maryann Kelly
IntuitiveServicesInsight.com
info@IntuitiveServicesInsight.com

YOUR MOMENT OF

Self-Awareness

Tap into the moment you received Level One attunement, no matter when it happened or how long ago it was. Look back at yourself with wiser, more intuitive eyes now. Remember yourself sitting there about to receive your first attunement. Remember and notice much more now. Write down the instant details of your awareness.

_____

_____

_____

_____

_____

_____

_____

_____

Second Degree Wisdom

The second degree directs healing to the mental and emotional spheres. Reiki Level II concentrates on negative thinking patterns, depression, happiness, deep ruts, relationships, communication, and the entire spectrum of human emotions. This degree also begins our awareness of healing across distances of time and space. We are given three of the five symbols—Sei He Kei, Cho Ku Rei, and Hon Sha Ze Sho Nen. You should have received instructions about each symbol's meaning, how each functions, and how to use each one.

You may have noticed that your own personal sense of life shifted mentally and emotionally. Some of these changes may have been quite subtle, while others may have been dramatic. Did this come as a surprise or did you expect it? Can you see the wisdom in the changes that happened in your life?

At this level, the Hon Sha Ze Sho Nen is studied and distant healing is introduced and practiced. Distance healing includes sending Reiki to someone on the other side of the world or from one end of your house to another. Distance Reiki may also happen when your hands are an inch above the skin of the person you are assisting. It includes healing earlier years in our life or situations that happened a week ago in our current life. Distance Reiki is used to heal our past lives, or what might be considered our karma. The lamp is cranked up to its next level of wattage and light when the student receives the second attunement.

Personal Story: Anne Ruthmann

Distance healing was a part of the Reiki II training and practice that surprised me the most. The level of my surprise was directly proportional to the level of skepticism I'd had around any of it actually working or being validated. To say the least, I was highly skeptical that any of it would do anything.

After spending so much time learning about Reiki I as a hands-on healing practice with all sorts of different hand positions and learning how to understand various sensations through the hands, to then be tasked with completely removing ourselves from having a physical client body in front of us or any immediate sensory experience just seemed like hocus pocus at first.

This is where practicing Reiki II with a group of people in person made a huge difference. We were able to try different techniques and share our experiences in ways that helped us understand what distance healing might feel like for the receiver/client and the sender/ Reiki practitioner. Since much of what Reiki is and can be is learned through practice and experience, it gave us more opportunities to understand what distance healing could do with people who already had a shared language of the various things we experienced in Reiki I.

When I was in the role of the Reiki distance healing client, the experience felt soft and relaxing, and I had a few mental impressions of beautiful moments and scenery. It was peaceful and soothing like a simple guided meditation, but no one was speaking to me or guiding me; it was all just happening as a moment of me sitting still, relaxing. That experience was great, but it didn't really sell me on the idea that anything was actually going on or that any kind of healing was taking place other than simple relaxation. Which was fine in and of itself, but it didn't do much to convince me that Reiki distance healing was really "working" or "doing anything" if that was the only experience I'd ever had with distance healing work.

However, I had another experience with distance healing work that did convince me. When I was the Reiki practitioner, I ended up receiving all sorts of information and insight about someone's physical energy body and energetic experiences that were later confirmed by the receiving client. How could I possibly know these things about this person without them ever telling me first? How was I able to sense issues that I'm not able to see or feel directly with my hands? Only after sharing what I experienced with several clients during the session, and having them confirm their awareness of the things I received intuitive guidance about, did I begin to think that maybe, just maybe, there's really some kind of truth in experiencing and practicing Reiki distance healing.

The more curious I became, the more I wanted to practice on people to see what kind of physical, emotional, and spiritual insights were possible to confirm through distance healing. The more experience and confirmation I had from various people I'd never even met in person, the more I began to understand that it wasn't just an imagined experience. Something was really happening and unfolding in that space of distance healing work.

Anne Ruthmann
www.anneruthmann.com
anneruthmann@gmail.com

YOUR MOMENT OF

Self-Awareness

Tap into the moment you received Level 2 no matter when it happened or how long ago it was. Please notice 1) your personal life changes and what happened within your soul as a result, and 2) your intuitive awareness now during distant healings. Do you realize now that you have been receiving intuitive information during distant Reiki? Write down the instant details of your awareness.

Third Degree Wisdom

Some master-teachers break this level into two parts. Part one often focuses on health and healing on the spiritual soul level, and the second part is about becoming a teacher of Reiki. Healing on the soul level is directed especially toward turning the work over to God, our guides, the collective wisdom, or the highest intelligence. Please use whatever term is most comfortable to you. I became aware that I felt less in charge of each Reiki session. I never really was in charge, and neither are you. Again, as discussed earlier in this book, we are mere vessels in healings on the earth plane.

An important reminder to you: We humans are vital links in the healing system. We healers are crucial links with the healers in the non-physical realms. Healing takes us all working as a team with other people, the earth, and the cosmos.

During the third degree, the last two symbols of the five are taught and the third attunement is given. *Click*, the light snaps open to the brightest wattage. Now the student becomes more keenly aware that she or he is a conduit for fine, fast electrical energy. Your instructor should encourage you at this level to allow the most divine and sacred healing guides and wise frequencies to surge through you without any hinderances.

YOUR MOMENT OF

Self-Awareness

I ask you to tap into the aliveness within you that is indeed your soul. Ask your soul to speak to you clearly. Ask what your soul wants and needs; your next step in accurately receiving intuitive wisdom for others and where your path is leading you. Write down the instant details of your awareness.

_____

_____

_____

_____

_____

_____

_____

_____

_____

_____

CHAPTER 12

Intuitive Reiki Healings

Reiki always assists and always heals, but healing will not materialize in one single way. Most people measure healing as the complete end of an illness or the complete avoidance of death. Reiki will not stop death if it is time to cross over into a new experience of living called death. We can offer Reiki before, during, and after the death transition. Healing may be the complete release of fear, allowing a readiness for death. It is a natural loving vibration that helps send us on our way to the brightest loving light of all. Healing can be a remission of cancer or quickly mending a fractured bone and everything in between.

Healing comes in all forms and constantly looks and feels different for every individual. Healing transforms the practitioners and the clients in an uncountable number of ways. We are only facilitators of healing. We are never the lone healer in any situation. In fact, the more we get out of the way and become the clearest, cleanest vessel of Reiki, the more profound the healing can be. It is impossible to define what a healing will be or what it will look like. I can only offer some simple steps to achieve the vast experiences of intense healing for others. The people you assist will then be able to tell you what you have done for them.

Specific Meaning of Color

One of the first intuitive impressions that you may notice during your healing sessions are colors. Earlier we talked about symbols as being more than black lines on white paper. Those symbols may transition from black lines in your thoughts or your mind's eye to colored lines. You will also experience different areas of the person's body changing colors during a session. You may sense the changes happening around or under your hands or within an organ or a section of the body.

When you perceive color, it is not random. You are sensing the aura, which is the aliveness within the body. That aliveness is in fact the soul of the individual. You are perceiving an eternal soul. That aliveness fluctuates with every single thought and every single emotion. Its energy vibrates not only with thoughts and emotions, but it also vibrates with our eternal story. You are witnessing the person's thrills, sorrows, joys, sadness, irritations, struggles, and the level of wisdom they have reached over eternity.

Color is only the visual layer of a spiritual being that is also in a human body. We are not separate from the non-physical realm. We are the non-physical and physical realm at the exact same time. Color equals intuitive information about that person.

You will notice that a person's colors are often different throughout their physical body. For example, their head may be bright yellow while at the same time their heart might be a dark red-brown and their big toe seems to have a black crack across it. As you send Reiki into their energy field and their physical body, these colors may dramatically change right before your eyes. This is the healing power of Reiki at work! So take note of the initial color and how it changes during the session. A bright, shiny color may become brighter, a darkened shade may lighten, or the foggy mist may lift out of their body and up into the atmosphere. You are simply the vessel for Reiki and the neutral intuitive observer of it all.

While each person is an individual, the following color chart offers you a foundational guideline of information about your client. Notice each color has a spectrum of positive and also negative traits.

Aura Color Chart

Red	Cellular health, energy, high temper, movement, extroversion
Light Red	Nervous, impulsive, passion, eroticism, sexuality, love
Dark Red	Will power, masculinity, rage, courage, suffering, leadership
Pink	Femininity, longings, sensitivity, emotional, softness
Brown	Egotism, addiction, disease, earthiness, unloving
Orange	Active intelligence, confident, expressive, warmth, joy of life, sex
Orange-Red	Taking action, pride, vanity, idealism, desire
Orange-Yellow	Sharp intellect, quick wit, industrious
Yellow	Clear, active thinking, likes their thinking abilities
Dark Yellow	Timid, thrift, restrictions, control needs
Gold	Devotion, higher inspiration, meditative state, authority, creative
Forest Green	Abundance, harvest, deep level of healing
Green	Growth, change, nature, devotion, neutral state, healing, harmony
Light Green	Sympathy, direct, possible deceit or lying

Blue	Introversion, solitude, truth, devotion to spirit, wisdom, prayer, writing
Light Blue	Softness, religious, reserved, struggle to mature
Indigo	Healing ability, morality, immersed in work, spiritual, mediumship
Turquoise	Giving Love to others in a healing capacity, expansion
Lavender	Mysticism, magic, overbearing, obsessions
Violet	Intuition, art, creativity, supernatural, imagination
Clear White	Eternal, forever, godlike
Milky White	Spirituality, higher consciousness, physical pain
Silver	Love about the Great Mother
Black	Protection, shielding, detached from senses, meditative
Gray	Duty, karma, resistance, depression

Four Important Keys About Color

1. Trust and believe that you just intuitively noticed color.
2. Understand that colors are fleeting moving energy and will not remain solid like globs of paint.
3. Notice how the colors change during the session.
4. Each color and each shade of color is not just color. It is detailed intuitive information.

YOUR MOMENT OF

Self-Awareness

If you have been working to convince yourself that you cannot see colors or auras, here is what I want you to do now. Ask three people for permission to practice with them, either at a distance or face to face. Then literally play and pretend that you instantly notice a color and its location. Notice that the colors may come as a word in your mind or a color in your mind's eye, or you may perceive color with your eyes open. It does not matter the pathway it comes on. What does matter is to play and always accept the most instant color that pops into your awareness and its location. Write down the instant details of your awareness.

Practice Person 1

_____

_____

_____

_____

_____

_____

_____

Practice Person 2

_____

_____

_____

_____

_____

_____

_____

Practice Person 3

_____

_____

_____

_____

_____

_____

_____

_____

Healing Characteristics of Color

Colors are often the first awareness that a new Reiki practitioner perceives in the non-physical realm. Color is frequencies of information, but they also carry healing properties. For example, if a symbol changes in your mind's eye from black lines to one of these colors, then the Reiki guides are sending that particular frequency into the recipient. If you begin to think or see one of these colors flow through your hands or begin to fill the person's body, then please honor that signal and allow yourself to be a clear channel for that particular healing frequency. These colors are at their finest healing level when they are clear, strong, pure, and shimmery. The following color vibrations have these healing characteristics:

Red – Brings vitality to area, builds up energy, improves health at a cellular level.

Orange – Decreases or eliminates toxins, increases ability to expel toxins, improves liver and kidney function.

Yellow – Builds a stronger sense of empowerment and individuality, fills emptiness, improves skin and bones.

Green – Renewal, regeneration, decongestant, detoxifying, breaks up blood clots, disinfectant, heals and opens the heart.

Blue – Decreases inflammation and infection, cools and soothes.

Purple/Violet – Breaks up density of physical/emotional restrictions or blockages, increases the effect of all levels of healing.

YOUR MOMENT OF Self-Awareness

What physical struggles are you dealing with in your own body? Place your hands on your own body and begin sending Reiki into that area of your body. Once you sense the Reiki flowing, then think and imagine one of the healing colors that relates to healing your struggle. Do not work hard, just imagine. Then also practice working with the healing colors for someone else. Write down the instant details of your awareness.

Self Practice

_____

_____

_____

_____

Practice Person

Personal Story: Cara Gallucci

I have been a Reiki practitioner for more than twenty-five years, and a meditator and meditation teacher for even longer than that. From the time I started working with people one-on-one as a meditation guide, I became aware that our energy fields interacted in a way that enhanced my intuition. As I entered into a meditative state with another person, I sometimes could sense what he or she was experiencing within. Because I worked with a Jungian technique of inner exploration, I would have said we were connecting through our deep unconscious minds, or the collective unconscious. When I learned Reiki, I found that the healing energy created a similar effect, allowing me to perceive things about my clients beyond any information they shared with me. Later, as a hypnotist, I learned how to create rapport with my clients in order to facilitate their receptivity, and in the process I once again experienced the inner sharing I had encountered through meditation and Reiki.

We are constantly exchanging energy with the people around us, and this process may become even more powerful through our intention to help, our use of Reiki symbols, meditative entrainment, the very act of touching another, and other methods. We can either choose to ignore and suppress this natural sharing of energy, or we can acknowledge and develop it to encourage healing.

Learning Reiki coincided with a healing crisis in my life that I didn't even know I was about to face. Maybe it was even the Reiki energy itself that helped me recognize the seriousness of symptoms I had already experienced for many years. I have a benign but unusual hereditary problem with my bones, and my earlier attempts to address my symptoms had been dismissed by doctors as just another part of my lifelong illness. I was told I would have to learn to live with the occasional pain, and I did.

But at the time I learned Reiki, I noticed the waists of my clothes were getting inexplicably tighter, even though I had lost a great deal of weight. Then I noticed a small, bony protuberance on my back a bit above my waist. Having just learned Reiki, I gave energy to this area through my hands as often as I could. Soon after, X-rays revealed a huge tumor made of bone—the size of a head of cauliflower, I was told. It was growing inside my rib cage like an iceberg, thrusting only a tip outside the back rib. My doctors could not believe that someone could have a tumor so large and appear to be as healthy as I looked!

During the weeks before I had surgery, I used Reiki on myself nightly. I believe it was all the good energy I received through Reiki, love, prayers, and my devotion that allowed me to fly through the surgery and recover in record time. Considering that my surgical incision went halfway around my body, that the tumor had grown into major organs, and that part of my liver and several ribs had to be removed, the nurses were amazed at how quickly I was able to be moved out of intensive care. I had no medical treatment other than surgical removal of the massive stage 4 malignancy, and I have been cancer-free ever since.

I have worked with all kinds of people in my practice. However, after this experience, I naturally attracted a number of people suffering from cancer. Most have pursued conventional medical treatments with Reiki and private instruction in meditation as adjunct therapies. Reiki makes an excellent accompaniment to conventional therapies. For example, Reiki before and after surgery reduces fear and helps a person to heal more quickly. It also relieves pain, surgical or otherwise. Administered before and after chemotherapy or radiation, Reiki can lessen or even prevent uncomfortable side effects.

Such was the case with one client of mine who was bedridden with a form of bone cancer. I went to his home to work on him as he lay in the hospital-style bed his family had installed for him. Before we began, this man had been through several rounds of chemotherapy, each of which had made him quite ill. When we met, he was wasted and painfully thin. During our first sessions, he was barely able to speak to me. But when he did speak, his eyes were bright and full of life. In my meditation, I asked whether I should be helping this man prepare for death, because from all appearances death seemed imminent. Always I was told, "*No!* He won't die of cancer." After a couple of years, he did die, but his doctor said he did not have cancer at that time.

Soon after we began our work together, it was time for him to receive more chemotherapy. This time, with Reiki, there were no side effects and he tolerated chemo surprisingly well, as his wife told me on more than one occasion. Both husband and wife were very grateful and wished they had started Reiki sooner.

A fascinating effect that both his wife and I observed was that whenever I gave Reiki to my client, all living beings in the house settled down. The cats, which before I started Reiki had been quite frisky, jumping on me and meowing, settled somewhere and napped. So did the inquisitive, barking dog. If any of the grandchildren were present, they went from noisy and active to quiet and still. And the wife, though always amazingly serene, noticed how much more relaxed and even drowsy she felt while I was doing Reiki in another room.

In working with clients over a long period of time, a bond forms that heightens my intuitive awareness of what might be happening with them. I had several such experiences with a young woman who had multiple myeloma, a disease that affects the bones and bone marrow. She had been given Prednisone, a steroid drug that caused her to gain weight and stop menstruating. Although she wanted to have children, her doctors told her she would most likely become sterile due to her treatments.

One day after I had worked with her, something prompted me to say, "Go home and rest. You are going to have a revelation." I forgot that strange message, but my client called me a few days later. While resting, she had become more and more upset. For some time before, she'd believed she was pregnant, but the doctors who examined her insisted she wasn't. She'd tried home pregnancy tests, but she spilled them. That afternoon, she tried one more self-test successfully and it told her she was pregnant. This time, her doctor confirmed she was four months along! The timing was crucial, because if it had been any earlier, her doctors would have pressed her to terminate the pregnancy for her own safety.

The night after she called me with that amazing story, I was watching the news on TV. A quick news-byte told me pregnancy hormones showed promise as a treatment for multiple myeloma, but of course, years of study were still needed. Hearing that brief story at that precise moment seemed almost as miraculous as my client's pregnancy. In a flash, I knew the pregnancy would stop my client's disease, and it did. She went into remission and gave birth to two beautiful children in the years before the cancer recurred, giving her two more reasons to continue fighting for her life.

Cara Gallucci
www.OmniStressRelief.com
781-724-2982

Did you get goose bumps? Do you truly realize the intense, profound, sensitive, subtle and sometimes not so subtle ways your Reiki healings are for another soul? There really are no words for it.

Specific Steps for Hands-On Intuitive Reiki

Here I offer consecutive steps as a summary to assist you in applying all that we have discussed so far.

1. Completely fill and saturate yourself with Reiki by thinking of the greatness of Reiki and at the same time deeply inhaling Reiki energy and its life force from the universe. Understand that your breathing is a pumping mechanism, and you are in charge of pumping up with Reiki first. Do not begin a session unless you have pumped up and filled yourself up completely. Never give your own energy to the individual.

2. Your eyes can be open or closed. Stop all thoughts of self. Direct all awareness to the person you are assisting.

3. Invite your Reiki spirit guide specialist to assist you specifically to heal the person you are about to assist. Turn everything over to Reiki and the specialists who are there for you and for your client.

4. In your mind ask your specialist to create a safe, secure, sacred space now for the healing work before you begin.

5. Verbally ask permission and tell the client that they do not lose control in any way. Remember, doing so will dramatically help the person to realize they are not losing control and allows them to relax and be able to absorb the energy even more. I also inform them that I will not be talking during the session, but I will answer their comments. Sense the person relax even more.

6. Feel the client actively receiving and literally soaking in the energy. They will have no need to create a protective barrier around them out of fear of the unknown.

7. Reiki and intuition will always feel like your imagination because you are working

with energy and it will not have the characteristics of physical earthly things, so it must feel like imagination.

8. Follow the directives from your spirit guide specialists for hand placements, symbols to use, etc.

9. Feel and sense everything about the universal life force coming into you and through you and into the recipient. Never give your energy to the session. Never allow the client's energy to come into you.

10. Notice everything that pops into your awareness through all of your intuitive pathways—thoughts, images, smells, tastes, physical signals your own body picks up about their body, auric colors, action scenes like a movie unfolding before your eyes.

11. Because you do not want to disturb the sacredness of the session, memorize the details of the intuitive insights so you can share it after the session.

12. When the session seems complete, ask the person to take their time to rise from the table. Tell them that you received some information about their energy and ask if they would like you to tell them about it. People are truly yearning for this type of help.

13. Verbally inform them and consider also drawing a picture of what you witnessed for them to take home. Ask if what you perceived made any sense to them. Do not try to interpret or explain what you intuitively received.

14. Finish each session with a good, positive closure. Ask your guides to build a perfect filter and then with your thoughts, pull all your personal energy that may have entered into the healing back through that cleansing filter. Feel that all of you has returned to you.

15. Be confident and trust everything that you receive because you are truly radiating the universal life force and universal love called Reiki.

YOUR MOMENT OF

Self-Awareness

Give Reiki sessions to three people. Practice the steps just described. Notice the details of the intuitive information that leaps into your awareness. Write down the instant details of your awareness.

Practice Person 1

_____

_____

_____

_____

_____

_____

_____

Practice Person 2

_____

_____

_____

_____

_____

_____

_____

Practice Person 3

_____

_____

_____

_____

_____

_____

_____

Specific Steps for Intuitive Distant Reiki

Realities exist beyond the physical world and beyond what our human minds can conceive. Healing energy instantly bolts across time and space. It is just as real as placing your hands on someone covered in a blanket in your healing room. Distance work is just as real and does not take any more time than placing your hands on someone covered in a blanket in your healing room. The receiver might be three thousand miles away or three miles away or on your table—the distance does not affect Reiki.

Ask for permission to send Reiki. There are a couple of different methods to make contact with the person you are concerned about. It can be as simple as literally calling or texting them and asking if it is alright to send them good wishes or good energy or prayers or Reiki. Use a term that you think they will be comfortable with. At this point in your Reiki career, it should not be about your comfort. You are opening and blossoming with Reiki and intuitive information and are becoming more convinced it is real and you are the real deal as well. (Saying that makes me smile.)

When asking for permission you might visualize the person giving you a smile or frown or turning to walk away or jumping up and down in happiness etc. You will always get a response that informs you about a refusal or acceptance. You might think that you just made it up, but you will receive a response. Maybe the response will be by hearing their voice or simply a "knowing." Do not deny a negative response. Honor the person's wishes, for you have not just imagined it. It is really their choice and you will perceive that choice accurately.

Make a commitment now that you will always honor a no. Do not try to justify in your mind that you know what is better for them and continue on with the session even though you know you received a refusal. In my experience with thousands of people, honoring a person's refusal will keep you from entering into a negative place. Forcing something on someone for their own good (what you have decided is for their own good) is not working from the purest light of Source. Remember that you can always ask the next day or the next, and one day you may receive an image in your mind's eye of a big smile on their face and you will know it is time.

Distant healing for one's current-life events. Here I offer consecutive steps as a summary to assist you in applying all that we have discussed for distant healing in one's current life.

1. Completely fill and saturate yourself with Reiki by thinking of the greatness of Reiki and at the same time deeply inhaling Reiki energy and life force from the Universe. Understand that your breathing is a pumping mechanism and you are in charge of pumping up with Reiki first. Do not begin a session unless you have pumped up and filled up.

2. Your eyes can be open or closed. Stop all thoughts of self. Direct all awareness to the person you are assisting no matter where the two of you are located.

3. Invite your Reiki spirit guide specialist to assist you specifically to heal the person you are about to assist. Turn everything over to Reiki and the specialists who are there for you and for your client.

4. Ask your specialist to create a safe, secure sacred space across the distance between you and your client.

5. Ask permission of the receiver to begin.

6. Actively use the Hon Sha Ze Sho Nen. You can think of the name of this symbol or visualize it. It will often, in your mind's eye, seem as if it covers the entire person you are working with.

7. Follow any directives from your specialty guide.

8. Never give your own energy to the session.

9. Notice everything that pops into your awareness through all of your intuitive pathways—thoughts, images, smells, tastes, physical signals your own body picks up about their body, auric colors, action scenes like a movie unfolding before your eyes.

10. Remember to program the Hon Sha Ze Sho Nen to continue sending Reiki in a rhythmic pulsing pattern into the client.

11. Finish each session with a good, positive closure. Ask your guides to build a perfect filter and then with your thoughts, pull all your personal energy back through that cleansing filter. Feel that all of you has returned to you.

12. Be confident and trust everything that you receive because you are truly radiating The Universal Life Force and Universal Love called Reiki.

YOUR MOMENT OF   Give yourself time now to send healing to your own current events in your life and then do the same steps to assist another person. Write down the instant details of your awareness.

Self-Awareness

Self Healing

_____

_____

_____

_____

_____

Practice Person

Distant healing for one's past events. Because each person's life is a continuum of moments and we are energy first and foremost, we are able to send Reiki healing back into our own past events or the past events of others we are assisting. Usually a highly emotional event—positive, negative, or traumatic—produces an ongoing connection to the past. That is why earlier life traumas may still affect our current lives. We travel through the continuum of time and space lugging around an unconscious weight.

Heartache and trauma are not the only energies that move with us. Profound healing also flows freely across time and space. Reiki can be sent back to painful memories to completely and permanently heal that particular moment. You and your clients will know the past event is healed when there is no longer any emotional impact from it. In fact, you or your client will only remember it as neutral information about your past. It will no longer feel painful. It will become an emotionless historical piece of information. Painful past events are soon understood as opportunities to learn and advance in wakeful consciousness. We always have that choice to heal our past, our present, and our future.

There are as many variations of distance healing experiences as there are people. Remember that simple and brief is just as powerful as slow and tedious. If you think the past will take a long time to heal then it will. If you know that it can heal instantly then it will. It is your confidence and your intent that makes the difference.

The scenario may begin in this way. Your client informs you that they cannot get a painful memory that happened in their earlier years out of their mind. They might even say that it haunts them. Another way people bring up a past event that needs healing is to say that they have a secret that no one knows. They do not need to tell you what it is for you to send Reiki to it. They do not need to tell you what the past event is for you to send Reiki to it. If they share it with you, simply listen and take these steps.

Here are the steps for the intuitive healing of earlier events in one's life.

1. Completely fill and saturate yourself with Reiki by thinking of the greatness of Reiki and at the same time deeply inhaling Reiki energy and life force from the universe. Understand that your breathing is a pumping mechanism and you are in charge of pumping up with Reiki first. Do not begin a session unless you have pumped up and filled up.

2. Your eyes can be open or closed. Stop all thoughts of self. Direct all awareness to the person you are assisting no matter where the two of you are located.

3. Invite your Reiki spirit guide specialist to assist you specifically to send healing to an earlier event in the earlier life of this person. Turn everything over to Reiki and the specialists who are there for you and for your client.

4. Ask your specialist to create a safe, secure sacred space around you, your client, and the earlier painful moment.

5. Ask permission from all people involved in the event. Take note: if you do not receive permission from any of the people involved in the painful event, then specifically send healing to the event itself and to your client's younger self. In other words, you are sending healing to the painful moment and to whatever happened in that specific second in time.

6. Place the Hon Sha Ze Sho Nen over your client and ask Reiki to go directly to the painful moment in your client's past. Ask your guide for the best pulsing wave sequence to program the distant symbol. Follow any directives you receive from your specialty guide.

7. Never give your own energy to the session.

8. Notice everything that pops into your awareness through all of your intuitive pathways—thoughts, images, smells, tastes, physical signals your own body picks up about their body, auric colors, action scenes like a movie unfolding before your eyes.

9. Finish each session with a good, positive closure. Ask your guides to build a perfect filter and then with your thoughts, pull all your personal energy back through that cleansing filter. Feel that all of you has returned to you.

10. Be confident and trust everything that you receive because you are truly radiating the universal life force and universal love called Reiki.

YOUR MOMENT OF

Self-Awareness

Send healing to earlier times in your own current life and then do the same steps to assist another person. Write down the instant details of your awareness.

Self Healing

_____

_____

_____

_____

_____

_____

_____

Practice Person

_____

_____

_____

_____

_____

_____

_____

CHAPTER 13
Reiki and the World Around You

Teaching Reiki and Intuition to Others

Even if you take the third degree, you are not required to teach Reiki. The student learns how to teach the three degrees and also how to give the attunement to others, but there is no obligation to teach it. Many, many people tell me that they are terribly afraid to teach and to stand in front of other people. In fact, all these worries led me to write *The Reiki Teacher's Manual* to give some structure and some confidence to potential teachers. I now offer this book as the next step, to assist you, as a practitioner or a teacher, to understand all the strange and sometimes weird and scary intuitive perceptions that Reiki opens us up to.

The true Reiki master is one who is mastering Reiki through experiencing Reiki. It is taking action with Reiki that makes the difference. You will intellectually learn about Reiki by reading about it and talking about it, but you must experience it to obtain that "knowing." Using Reiki on a daily basis increases the ability to build up, hold within, and finally transmit the energy into another.

During an attunement, the teacher's energy merges with the student's aura. The teacher's field is already imprinted with the symbols, and the energy in general is accentuated by the teacher constantly being a vessel for Reiki. As the instructor draws the symbols into the student's field, an electromagnetic transference sparks an awakening on many levels for both of you at that moment. The teacher receives but is more of a wide-open vessel for the student, who has an opportunity to receive.

Notice two key details that I just mentioned.

Key 1 I did not say that the master-teacher takes on the student's karma and makes it their own. The teacher must set a powerful clear intent to never take on the student's burdens or energy density. The teacher must completely fill their field with Reiki until it seems that you might pop at any second and then allow Reiki to burst open as you give the attunement to the student.

Key 2 Teach the student before each attunement that it is completely their responsibility to allow the attunement to enter into their field. This is so important. Do you see the importance here? It is never the teacher's failure if the student does not fully receive the attunement. It is also up to the student to allow the release of all the energetic burdens they are carrying. This is a primary concept to teach to each student to prepare them for the attunement. Whatever is then received but also released by the student is sent out into the Universe.

It is up to the student to allow the full effect to happen, because the master-teacher cannot force the attunement and Reiki will not force it either. Our thoughts are so powerful, and this is still a realm of choice. It is always the student's responsibility for his or her own level of acceptance. Just like all of life, the attunement can be blocked or resisted by the student.

When completely accepted by the student, a rejuvenation releases obstructions or blockages. The natural circuitry in the human body flows more freely. The energy that is generated by the chakras surges through the meridian lines and radiates outward. It is thought that even the DNA, our genetic coding, is altered and improved. The wide-open student can feel a level of empowerment. There may not be any words for this feeling, although sometimes there is an emotional release of tears or even sobbing, or there may be a burst of laughter or a great nonverbal silence.

And then the intuitive wisdom either begins or increases exponentially. I was already very intuitively aware, but it was after my first attunement that I began perceiving directly into each person's energy field and down within their physical body like an X-ray machine. This book is meant to help prepare and assist all the Reiki practitioners and master-teachers out there. The world is truly more than the physical earth that we see around us. Everything is energy and the non-physical realm is just as alive, active, and real as the physical realm.

Please, as an instructor, share your intuitive experiences with your students. Do not just share the unusual or strange perceptions. Make sure that you share the stunningly beautiful images of your client's dark blockages bursting opening with a glow like that of the sun. Share your stories of client's tears of release as you send Reiki deep into their heart. Describe the pain that you witness rising up and out of your clients. Share with them what you have noticed about stepping out of the way and allowing the master-teacher specialty guides to lead the session. Explain to them that the non-physical world is opening up to them and their life is enriched with this level of wisdom for themselves and for the people they help along the way.

Personal Story: Jenni Rozevink

My first experience with Reiki was seemingly by chance. I was on vacation with a friend and we wanted a psychic reading. The only provider on the island did not feel right to either of us. After a few Google searches, we found a shop forty minutes away offering many services. One service was Reiki. Neither of us had ever heard of it before, but a quick conversation with the owner and we felt confident in our decision to try it. Anyways, it was only fifteen dollars and fifteen minutes of our time. What could go wrong with that? Nothing!

It was absolutely magical. Life changing for me, actually. I felt this miracle mixture of emotions and physical sensations—grounded, serene, calm, but energized and fully present in my body. Which at the time was a true feat of achievement. From that one short experience with Reiki, I decided I just had to know how to do it for myself.

Thankfully I found a Reiki master offering attunements much closer to home. On a Saturday late in March of 2016, I had my second life-altering experience with Reiki. It was toward the end of the class and to my great dismay, my turn to hop on the table. I was dreading it. I knew it would ultimately be beneficial, but it was also a challenge. Throughout the day I had the intuitive knowing that it was going to cause a huge release of intense emotion. Oh boy, did it!

Now, something you need to know is that I've always been intuitive. I've always just known things and had feelings. I couldn't always explain where they were coming from or how or why I knew something. I just did. I have also always spent a lot of time in emotional and mental spaces. I'm talking *gobs* of time just feeling and thinking. What I had not done, and am still working on, is being present and fully connected to my physical being.

Well that afternoon, all aspects of me merged into one via a humbling, surprising, and incredibly moving experience. I had been on the table mere minutes before the first classmate got their hand directly over my heart chakra and an intense wave—more like a drowning of sorrow—exploded and engulfed me. In a logical way it made sense. There had been many moments of severe emotional pain and mental anguish. I had no idea that it could and did affect my physical body, my actual heart. I wish I could say I was beside myself at that moment, but I was fully in my being, experiencing the full weight and release of it. In two separate experiences, short in duration, Reiki had firmly connected all of me. All of my being, all of my awareness and senses, at once. That Reiki I attunement had led me straight to the path of coming home to myself, acknowledging all aspects of myself and my abilities.

Since then, intuitive knowings have always been present in my Reiki and medical intuition practice. Knowings, symbols, metaphors, and psychical sensations are all normal and welcome aspects to my work. Being intuitive is now so immersed in my being, I have no idea how I could ever be without it. It is what I measure all things against. Divine guidance helps immensely, but my intuitive being is my true essence, the piece of me that is a piece of God and oneness with all of creation. It is how I know what I know is accurate and what behaviors and actions are ethical. It is how I sense everything in relation to myself, and in relation to all of the worlds. It allows me to move through all experiences in an efficient and respectful manner.

I received my Reiki Master attunement a year and three months after Level I. In between those dates and since then I have traveled through time, space, and various realities and realms, guided by my intuition to help myself and others become more whole and present and firmly find their connection to universal energy life force. It would not be possible or safe without the synergistic combining of all aspects of myself—the mental, emotional, spiritual, physical, and intuitive self. Something Reiki first powerfully, efficiently, and practically effortlessly provided for me to experience.

I am beyond grateful for the energy practice of Reiki and all the practitioners everywhere that have decided to participate in it and to follow their paths with integrity, strength, and grace. I look forward eagerly as I get ready to attune my first batch of Reiki practitioners. And I will, without a doubt, include how intuitive knowings and experiences go hand in hand with the practice of Reiki.

Jenni Rozevink
selenitesage@gmail.com
419-980-6513

Personal Story: Sheri Woxland

I took my first Reiki class in 2003. I remember my teacher telling me that you did not have to even be thinking about Reiki as you were doing a session because Reiki energy knows exactly where to go in the body of the client. She said that you could be thinking about your grocery list, or what you planned on doing that night. It was at that moment that I discounted Reiki as a valid healing modality. I thought, "I understand that the Reiki energy can go where it needs to in a person's body, but there needs to be some intention on the practitioner's part to create a truly healing atmosphere."

Over the next couple of years, I took Level II and Level III hoping to find more meaning, but I did very little with using Reiki. It wasn't until I moved to Kansas City and decided that I wanted to teach Reiki myself that things began to change. I knew that I wanted to do it differently than how I was taught.

I had four students for my first class and I was scared! What did I really know? Could I instill in them the true meaning of Reiki and of healing and the energy of love? I did the class in three-day segments over a three-week period of time. I wanted the students to have the time to practice on other people and see how the energy felt to them. I wanted them to get feedback from the people that they worked on so that they could realize that what they were doing made a difference. I wanted them to be able to share their experiences with the other students and discuss how the Reiki energy worked for them.

I taught both the Eastern and Western ways of Reiki. I wanted them to know that they could do either, or both. There is a time and a place for both. I instilled in each student the importance of having a clear intent for healing during the session. I had the students practice feeling the energy in whatever way they sensed it and to notice the subtle differences in energy. I emphasized the importance of being present during the session, even though the Reiki energy knows exactly where it needs to go.

The most surprising experience that I had during the teaching process occurred during the attunements. After I had set up the room and prepared it for the students, I asked the Reiki masters and guides to enter and be with the students during their attunement. And then, there they were! Each chair was occupied by a Reiki guide. I looked in amazement, then took the time to thank each of them for coming. I knew that it was important to note which guide was in each chair so that I could tell the student who sat there, who had shown up for them. When I shared with each student, it was a very powerful experience. The students were amazed with how the guide that came for each of them was exactly the one that they needed or had experienced before.

I am very grateful for that wonderful day when my faith in Reiki really came full circle. I am grateful for the students and the guides and masters and for the wonderful healing modality called Reiki!

Sheri Woxland
www.atthehealingplace.com
Sheri@atthehealingplace.com

When we teach Reiki we commit to and pledge a life of kindness, non-judgment, and grace to the physical and non-physical life of this universe.

YOUR MOMENT OF

Self-Awareness

Are you a teacher now or hope to be soon? Speak to yourself right now about any struggles you have experienced during this learning process offered in this book. Then notice what your intuitive guidance is telling you now. Write down the instant details of your awareness.

_____

_____

_____

_____

_____

_____

_____

_____

Intuitive Reiki for the World Around You

If you think that there are limits for using Reiki, those limits are only in your mind. Reiki is the life force of the Universe, and the Universe has no end and it has no limits. There is no end to what you can use Reiki for.

Place your hands on your washer and dryer. Place your hands on your bicycle, your car, or the oven in your kitchen. What we usually think of as inanimate objects, ones made of metal, wood or plastic, are made up of vibrating molecules too. There is a level of aliveness in everything. Do you know that you can Reiki your home and the land it is on? You can Reiki other buildings such as schools, businesses, courthouses, or government buildings. Place your hands on your houseplants, your garden, your food, your vitamins, and even your prescription medications. It will all respond to your healing hands and what is good and positive in them will be enhanced for you with Reiki.

The healer can also Reiki certain locations where people have been injured or have died. Railroad tracks or intersections are areas that can be healed. Airports and mountain cliffs are other examples of areas that will respond to healing. Send Reiki to specific countries or areas of violence. Send Reiki to the entire globe we call earth. Open all the doors of your mind and allow Reiki to flow through you.

Personal Story: Cheryl F. Meisterman, PhD, LISW-S

My dear neighbor was diagnosed with fourth stage cancer in October 2003 shortly after her mother passed from cancer. I began offering her Reiki a month before her chemo began. Once a week, I would enter her room and she would play some meditative music while I gave her a Reiki treatment and we chatted. By the time of her first chemo, she was reclassified as having third stage cancer. She was given an eight-year life expectancy, with little chance for a cure.

I continued to offer weekly sessions for the first three years, then we shared sessions twice a month. About four years ago, she had a stem cell transplant and I was given permission to continue giving Reiki in the hospital, although visitors were limited due to her vulnerable health condition. She claims her stress is relieved and her sleep improves after a treatment.

Each fall, as she is able, she has treated me to a concert and/or a dinner, for our energy exchange. Some years, it was difficult for her to walk or to have the stamina to participate. This is our fifteenth year in celebration of her life sharing Reiki. We now celebrate her two birthdays, one when she was born and the other the anniversary day of her transplant. We will be dancing to Phil Collins together this October, Spirit willing.

I give myself Reiki treatments five mornings a week, readying myself for work. As a psychologist, I want to be as in tune as I can be, so I am available to the clients that entrust me with their stories. Reiki aids me in centering and healing and provides a reminder that I am just a conduit.

I have given Reiki sessions to aid friends and family in their transitions from this physical life and babies who are beginning their lives here. My husband, a naysayer, was supposed to have surgery on his finger, but after treating his hand while we watched TV over a week, about thirty minutes each night, he did not need the surgery. He softened his stance on Reiki after that experience and has supported me in sharing Reiki with others.

Reiki has enhanced my life in all ways. I am grateful and humbled.

Cheryl F. Meisterman, PhD, LISW-S

Important Truths about Reiki and Intuition

1. Intuition is simply receiving information that is everywhere around us.

2. Reiki is the most precious healing love energy that is everywhere around us.

3. We are immersed in waves of information and love every second of every day.

4. Intuition is a natural mechanism of perceiving; it is not magical or mystical.

5. Reiki is a natural vibration of the universe.

6. Intuition and Reiki will always feel like they occur in your imagination because both are non-physical.

7. Intuitive Reiki is sensing, perceiving, and becoming the clearest vessel possible.

8. Intuition is steady, calm, whispery, and will consistently give you the same information over and over again about a single topic/issue.

9. Intuition utilizes all of our physical senses plus the sixth sense of knowing.

10. Focus on sensing the process of Reiki and step more and more out of the way of Reiki and your spirit guide specialist.

11. Absolutely trust what you receive no matter what, even if you do not understand it.

12. Do not interpret what you receive. The receiver will tell you what it means to them.

13. You are an antenna for intuition and a vessel for Reiki all at the same time.

14. Like an antenna, do not work to receive. Receive effortlessly.

15. Incorporate Reiki and intuition to enrich your daily life and be playful with it.

Practice today, tomorrow, and every day and every
moment beyond that moment. When your hands
touch something, anything, it becomes a
Reiki moment for healing and an intuitive moment
to receive special insights from
the universe.

You are and always have been the union of
healing and wisdom.

Now, be all you are meant to be.

Create Your Own Personal Story

Contact the Contributors

I am delighted, humbled, and honored to each of the following people who have contributed their Reiki story to this book. They opened up their lives to you as they told their personal stories. They have offered their contact information for you.

Jennifer Allgier: minusan@aol.com

Tammy Barton: www.AtTheHealingPlace.com; Tammy@AtTheHealingPlace.com

Jenny Chen: http://www.serenelylove.com

Cara Gallucci: www.OmniStressRelief.com; (781) 724-2982

Tina M. Horton, CMT: tinahorton.ps@gmail.com (260) 908-0976

Lori Irvin, Medical Intuitive: ZSourceConnection.com; Lorredd@hotmail.com

Maryann Kelly: IntuitiveServicesInsight.com; info@IntuitiveServicesInsight.com

Heather McCutcheon: www.ReikiBrigade.org; heather@reikibrigade.org

Elise Mori: www.lotusforest.net

Donna Parsons: soulsurge9@gmail.com

Lisa Rathore, RN: reikilove02@gmail.com

Julie Rebensdorf, MA, LSW: julierebensdorf@yahoo.com

Jenni Rozevink: selenitesage@gmail.com; (419) 980-6513

Anne Ruthmann: www.anneruthmann.com; anneruthmann@gmail.com

Rev. Dr. Michelle Walker, DNP: EmpoweredWellness.org; DrWalkerEmpoweredWellness@gmail.com

Sheri Woxland: www.atthehealingplace.com; Sheri@atthehealingplace.com

About the Author

TINA M. ZION is a fourth generation intuitive medium, specializing in medical intuition and teaching it internationally. She has worked in the mental health field as a registered nurse with a national board specialty certification in mental health nursing from the American Nurses Credentialing Association. Tina is a Gestalt trained counselor, graduating from the Indianapolis Gestalt Institute in 1997. She received her certification in clinical hypnotherapy from the American Council of Hypnotist Examiners in 1985, specializing in past life regressions and certified through the Michael Newton Institute. Tina is the internationally known bestselling author of *The Reiki Teacher's Manual, Become a Medical Intuitive,* and *Advanced Medical Intuition.* She is a contributing author in Newton's book, *Memories of the Afterlife.*

Tina no longer offers readings. Her private practice now focuses completely on teaching medical intuition through teleconferences, workshops, and individual mentoring sessions. Tina teaches her medical intuition workshop in Canada, the UK, Europe, New Zealand, Australia, and throughout the US.

Visit her website at www.tinazion.com

About the Author